ADVICE
FROM THE
LOTUS-BORN

A COLLECTION OF PADMASAMBHAVA'S ADVICE
TO THE DAKINI YESHE TSOGYAL AND OTHER CLOSE DISCIPLES
FROM THE TERMA TREASURE REVELATIONS OF
NYANG RAL NYIMA ÖZER,
GURU CHÖWANG,
PEMA LEDREL TSAL,
SANGYE LINGPA,
RIGDZIN GÖDEM,
& CHOKGYUR LINGPA

INTRODUCTORY TEACHING BY H. E. TULKU URGYEN RINPOCHE
TRANSLATED FROM THE TIBETAN BY ERIK PEMA KUNSANG
EDITED BY MARCIA BINDER SCHMIDT

RANGJUNG YESHE PUBLICATIONS
Boudhanath, Århus & Hong Kong

RANGJUNG YESHE PUBLICATIONS
FLAT 2C HATTAN PLACE
1A PO SHAN ROAD, HONG KONG

ADDRESS LETTERS TO:

RANGJUNG YESHE PUBLICATIONS
KA-NYING SHEDRUB LING MONASTERY
P.O. BOX 1200, KATHMANDU, NEPAL

PUBLICATION DATA:

PADMASAMBHAVA, YESHE TSOGYAL, NYANG RAL NYIMA ÖZER, GURU CHÖWANG, PEMA
LEDREL TSAL, SANGYE LINGPA, RIGDZIN GÖDEM, AND CHOKGYUR LINGPA.
FOREWORD BY TULKU URGYEN RINPOCHE (B. 1920). TRANSLATED FROM THE TIBETAN BY
ERIK PEMA KUNSANG (ERIK HEIN SCHMIDT). EDITED BY MARCIA BINDER SCHMIDT AND
KERRY MORAN.
FIRST ED.
TITLE: ADVICE FROM THE LOTUS-BORN, VOL. I.
ISBN 962-7341-20-7 (PBK.)
1. EXTRACTS FROM JO MO ZHUS LAN, MNGA' BDAG NYANG GI DMAR KHRID, DGONGS PA
ZANG THAL, BLA MA DGONGS 'DUS, MCHOG GLING GTER GSAR & MKHA' 'GRO SNYING THIG.
2. MAHAYANA AND VAJRAYANA — TRADITION OF PITH INSTRUCTIONS. 3. BUDDHISM —
TIBET. I. TITLE.

COVER PICTURE COURTESY OF ORGYEN TOBGYAL RINPOCHE

COVER PHOTO: GRAHAM SUNSTEIN

"These teachings are the central advice of the collected words of Padmasambhava, the great nirmanakaya master. They are words from his heart, meant to be personally practiced. Please keep this in mind!"

Yeshe Tsogyal

THE PRECIOUS GARLAND OF THE SUBLIME PATH
Gampopa
RAINBOW PAINTING
Tulku Urgyen Rinpoche
ADVICE FROM THE LOTUS-BORN MASTER
Padmasambhava
KING OF SAMADHI
Thrangu Rinpoche
THE UNION OF MAHAMUDRA AND DZOGCHEN
Chökyi Nyima Rinpoche
MIRROR OF MINDFULNESS
Tsele Natsok Rangdröl
BUDDHA NATURE
Khenchen Thrangu Rinpoche
REPEATING THE WORDS OF THE BUDDHA
Tulku Urgyen Rinpoche
SONG OF KARMAPA
Chökyi Nyima Rinpoche
EMPOWERMENT
Tsele Natsok Rangdröl
BARDO GUIDEBOOK
Chökyi Nyima Rinpoche
LIFE AND TEACHINGS OF CHOKGYUR LINGPA
Orgyen Tobgyal Rinpoche

FROM SHAMBHALA PUBLICATIONS:

LAMP OF MAHAMUDRA
Tsele Natsok Rangdröl
DAKINI TEACHINGS
Padmasambhava
THE LOTUS-BORN
Yeshe Tsogyal
LIGHT OF WISDOM
Padmasambhava and Jamgön Kongtrül

CONTENTS

FOREWORD

⁂

THE TEACHINGS INCLUDED IN *Advice from the Lotus-Born* were spoken directly by Padmasambhava to his close disciples in Tibet. Primarily they were given in response to questions from Lady Tsogyal, the princess of Kharchen, who wrote them down and concealed them as a precious *terma* treasure to be revealed many centuries later. Almost every chapter mentions that these instructions were given for the benefit of practitioners of future generations, and often they include the words: "May this meet with all worthy and destined people in the future!"

Advice from the Lotus-Born is a companion volume to *Dakini Teachings* (Shambhala Publications, 1989), and part of an ongoing effort to present the teachings of Padmasambhava for application by modern-day practitioners. Padmasambhava is the great master who established Buddhism in Tibet during the latter part of the eighth century. *The Lotus-Born* (Shambhala Publications, 1993) contains the details of his life.

Tulku Urgyen Rinpoche expressed the conviction that an English translation of these precious teachings would bring great benefit. He asked me to seek out and select the most profound instructions involving topics different from those presented in *Dakini Teachings*.

This volume containing the oral advice of Vajrayana's most outstanding master was collected from various terma teachings. While these revelations span many centuries and were revealed by different people at different places, their language and grammatical style are almost identical.

The material presented here represents only a fraction of the immense body of terma treasures revealed over the last millennium. This book was compiled from the following sources: Rigdzin Gödem's *Gongpa Sangtal*, Nyang Ral's *Martri*, Sangye Lingpa's *Lama Gongdü*, *Tongwa Dönden* (a compilation), Pema Ledrel Tsal's *Khandro Nyingtig*, and the *Chokling Tersar* of Chokgyur Lingpa.

The first chapter, entitled the *Jewel Spike Testament*, and the sixth and longest chapter, the *Treasury of Precious Jewels*, are taken from the famous *Gongpa Sangtal*, a cycle of terma teachings revealed by Rigdzin Gödem (1337-1408), the master of the Jangter or 'northern terma' tradition of the Nyingma school. Rigdzin Gödem literally means 'the vidyadhara with the vulture feather'; he received this name because three vulture feathers grew from his head when he was twelve years old, and five more when he was twenty-four. A reincarnation of Dorje Dudjom of Nanam, one of the nine close Tibetan disciples of Padmasambhava, he is also counted among the five king-like tertöns.

Gongpa Sangtal is an abbreviation of 'Showing Directly the Realization of Samantabhadra,' the primordial buddha. This collection of teachings also contains the renowned 'Aspiration of Samantabhadra.' *Gongpa Sangtal* consists of five sections; these chapters belong to the one called *Kadag Rangjung Rangshar*, 'self-existing and self-manifest primordial purity.'

The second major source is Nyang Ral's *Martri*, the 'Direct Instructions' of Padmasambhava revealed by the great master Nyang Ral Nyima Özer (1124-1192). In *Dakini Teachings* I briefly described Nyang Ral's life. This set of teachings was included by Jamgön Kongtrül (1813-1899) in *Rinchen Terdzö*, a renowned collection of terma teachings known as the *Precious Treasury of Termas*.

The third source is *Lama Gongdü*, revealed by Sangye Lingpa (1340-1396). The name means the 'embodied realization of the master' (Padmasambhava). Sangye Lingpa was a reincarnation of the second son of King Trisong Deutsen (790-844), and is counted among the Eight Lingpas or major tertöns. His principal revelation was the massive *Lama Gongdü* cycle of termas in 18 volumes of approximately 700 pages each, and the *Kathang Sertreng*, the extensive biography of Padmasambhava known as the *Golden Chronicles*.

Tongwa Dönden means 'meaningful to behold,' and is a biography of Padmasambhava compiled from three major sources: the Katang chronicles revealed by Orgyen Lingpa (1329-1360/67), Nyang Ral (1124-1192), and Guru Chöwang (1212-1270). Consisting of 274 large block-print folios, this manuscript was found in the library of Shechen Tennyi Dargye Ling in Boudhanath. The colophon mentions that it includes material from: 1) the *Extensive Biography* of the Great Master of Uddiyana, revealed by Orgyen Lingpa from the supreme place of the Crystal Cave of Yarlung; 2) the *Testament of Padma*, revealed by the great tertön Nyang Ral; 3) the *Biography of 45 Deeds*, composed by Princess Mandarava and condensed into the *Biography of 11 Deeds* by Guru Chöwang, the tertön of Lhodrak; and 4) separate instructions, various replies to questions, and prophecies from the *Lama Gongdü* cycle of Sangye Lingpa.

As the fourth source, I used a chapter from Pema Ledrel Tsal's *Khandro Nyingtig*, the 'Heart Essence of the Dakinis.' Padmasambhava concealed his teachings on the Innermost Unexcelled Cycle of the Great Perfection to be revealed in the future as *Khandro Nyingtig*. The tertön of this important cycle was Pema Ledrel Tsal (1291-1315/9), a reincarnation of Princess Pema Sal, the daughter of King Trisong Deutsen. His immediate rebirth was as the illustrious master Longchen Rabjam (1308-1363) followed by Pema Lingpa (1445-1521). In recent years this master incarnated as Khenpo Ngakchung, alias Ngawang Palsang (1879-1941), who also used the name Pema Ledrel Tsal.

Lastly, the *Aspiration of the Vajradhatu Mandala* is the single most important chant of good wishes in the *Chokling Tersar*. It is recited from memory at the end of almost any spiritual gathering in the Kagyü and Nyingma traditions. The *Chokling Tersar*, the 'New Terma Treasures of Chokgyur Lingpa' (1829-1870), were discovered by the great tertön and his two close associates Jamyang Khyentse Wangpo (1820-1892) and Jamgön Kongtrül the First (1813-1899).

Thanks to His Eminence Tulku Urgyen Rinpoche, who upholds the heart of Padmasambhava's teachings, for kindly explaining any question I had and for his profound instructions illuminating the depth of the view presented in this book; and to Chökyi Nyima Rinpoche for extensively teaching the Dharma over the years, including two seminars covering questions and answers between Padmasambhava and Yeshe Tsogyal.

Lastly, I rejoice in the fact that these translations were completed at the Asura Cave Temple on the tenth day of the lunar month, a day on which Padmasambhava promised to come from his pure land, the Glorious Copper-colored Mountain, to bless whoever calls upon him. May these precious teachings deeply inspire whoever reads them!

Erik Pema Kunsang
Nagi Gompa, 1994

INTRODUCTORY
TEACHING

❧

THE TEACHINGS CONTAINED IN *Advice from the Lotus-Born* belong to a style called *martri* or 'direct instructions'. *Martri* means personal advice given from the heart and taught in a clear and direct way, revealing the most intimate and treasured secrets. Often such advice is imparted only to one disciple at a time. Padmasambhava's direct instructions condense the essential meaning of the tantras of Mahayoga, the scriptures of Anu Yoga, and the pith instructions of Ati Yoga.

There is a saying that "When the flames of the dark age rage rampantly, the teachings of the vajra vehicle of Secret Mantra will blaze forth like wildfire." Padmasambhava is the primary master of Secret Mantra and he appears in that role accompanying each and every one of the thousand buddhas of this aeon.

My root guru Samten Gyatso often said, "Look closely and see how amazing Padmasambhava's terma teachings are! Compare terma revelations with any other treatise and see their unique quality. The reason is that primarily they were composed by Padmasambhava himself. The beauty of their prose is astounding!"

Samten Gyatso also said, "It is very difficult for anyone to compose literature of such beauty and depth as the prose found in terma practices. Unlike the treatises of merely learned people, each word can be understood on increasingly deeper levels. That is the special quality of Padmasambhava's vajra speech." My teacher would exclaim how he always marveled at Padmasambhava's words! Samten Gyatso was extremely erudite and had studied vast quantities of literature; even so, he was always able to find many different levels of meaning in Padmasambhava's teachings. "When you read the teachings of Padmasambhava, you inevitably feel faith and devotion," he said. "You cannot help but surrender yourself with complete confidence!" Samten Gyatso had incredible faith in Padmasambhava. He often said, "There is no one greater than Padmasambhava. Of course, Buddha Shakyamuni is the root, but Padmasambhava is the one who made the Vajrayana teachings spread and flourish throughout India and especially in Tibet."

We see that similarly worded teachings appear in the revelations of several tertöns. The reason is they are the unmistaken speech of Padmasambhava deciphered from symbolic script. One need not harbor any doubts. For instance, the *Seven Line Supplication* starting with "On the northwest border of the land of Uddiyana ..." appears in numerous different termas; the different revealers tapped the same source.

"The great authentic tertöns were amazing!", Samten Gyatso said. "Such masters as Nyang Ral, Guru Chöwang, and Rigdzin Gödem were truly incredible!" The first two tertön masters, Nyang Ral and Guru Chöwang, were known as the Two Tertön Kings, and the other hundred tertöns are described as their attendants. There are also the Three Eminent Tertöns, the Eight Lingpas, the 25 major tertöns and so forth, all of them of equal importance. But among the 108 tertöns, the main ones are the Two Tertön Kings: Nyang Ral Nyima Özer and Guru Chöwang. "None are greater than those two!", he said. The first among all tertöns was known as Sangye Lama, who, by the way, is not the same as Sangye Lingpa. I'm not familiar with the details of the various biographies; I only know that they were outstanding.

When Dzongsar Khyentse Chökyi Lodrö was staying in Gangtok, I had the fortune to visit him every morning for 25 days to ask many different questions. At that time his health was good, and as he was in semi-retreat he did not receive visitors. But because I was one of the descendants of Chokgyur Lingpa, he showed me special kindness and called me to visit. Often he was alone, without any attendant whatsoever.

One day I exposed my ignorance and asked, "People like myself who don't know anything have a hard time discerning which among all the termas on the deities of the Three Roots revealed by the Two Tertön Kings and the other 108 tertöns contained in the *Rinchen Terdzö* are the most important. We are like children picking flowers in a huge meadow, trying to choose the most beautiful. Which do you consider the most important?" He replied, "For the guru aspect, there is none greater than Guru Chöwang's *The Tenth Day Practice in Eight Chapters*. It is the sovereign among all types of guru sadhana. For the *yidam* aspect, Padmasambhava taught the *Eight Sadhana Teachings* and Nyang Ral's version is eminent. For the dakini aspect, Nyang's *Tröma Nagmo* is foremost. These three are the most important among all termas revelations." Guru Chöwang's *The Tenth Day Practice in Eight Chapters* is based on the form of Padmasambhava known as *Lama Sangdü*, the 'master who embodies all secrets.' There were three major versions of the Eight Sadhana Teachings. Among all the various dakini practices, Nyang's *Tröma Nagmo*, a black, wrathful form of Vajra Yogini, is extremely profound.

When I asked, "What should I personally practice?", Dzongsar Khyentse told me "Take the *Tukdrub Barchey Künsel* as your particular practice! Among the termas of Chokgyur Lingpa, the *Barchey Künsel* cycle is incredibly deep and was revealed without any hindrance. When obstacles are removed, accomplishment occurs spontaneously, so focus on that practice!"

"Who should I regard as the guru?", I asked. Dzongsar Khyentse replied, "Supplicate Chokgyur Lingpa! That will be sufficient! There is nothing incomplete in that; he will suffice as the guru aspect!"

Then I asked, "Which Dzogchen practice should I focus on?" Again Dzongsar Khyentse said, "You should practice *Kunzang Tuktig*! This period is the time when the two cycles *Kunzang Tuktig* and *Chetsün Nyingtig* will influence people. Each age has its particular teaching of the Great Perfection especially meant for that time. In an earlier age the most widely renowned was *Nyingtig Yabzhi*; later came Rigdzin Gödem's *Gongpa Sangtal* and Dorje Lingpa's *Tawa Long-yang*; then the *Könchok Chidü* cycle of Jatsön Nyingpo. Each terma came at its own particular time."

In this respect Samten Gyatso concurred: "Padmasambhava is exalted because before he left Tibet he concealed, for the practitioners of every century, an abundance of termas containing teachings, precious stones, and sacred articles. The tertöns who later appeared to reveal these terma treasures were blessed by Padmasambhava, and sent after receiving empowerment and reading transmission of the complete lineage. These days some intellectuals object, saying

'Tertöns probably don't possess the unbroken lineage of empowerment and reading transmission from Padmasambhava for their teachings. They just dig up a few articles they themselves hid!' In fact, every tertön has already received the complete transmission through Padmasambhava's blessings in an authentic way that is far superior to the superficial way empowerments and transmissions are frequently given, often with only a resemblance of blessings. All the great tertöns are masters who in body, speech and mind are blessed and empowered personally by Padmasambhava. To claim they didn't have transmission is childish. Such statements demonstrate the speaker's ignorance of the traditional seven ways of transmission. The terma teachings are amazingly profound, and are concealed within the treasure chest of the 'four modes and six limits.' There is much of depth to explore if you are interested."

From childhood, a great tertön is unlike an ordinary child. He has pure visions of deities, and realization overflows from within. Tertöns are not like us ordinary people who must follow the gradual path of study and practice. Ordinary people don't have instantaneous realization!

It is quite a few centuries since Padmasambhava lived, but through his great kindness he concealed innumerable termas for the benefit of future beings — within solid rock, in lakes, even within space. Thinking of this immense kindness evokes awe. Yet, there are people who can't even appreciate this kindness.

When the time came for the different terma teachings to be revealed, great tertöns would appear in this world. They were able to dive into lakes, fly up to impossible locations in caves and take objects out of solid rock.

My grandmother, who was the daughter of Chokgyur Lingpa, witnessed this, and later told me, "When the rock opened up, it looked like the anus of a cow; the rock became soft and just poured out to reveal a cavity containing the terma. Often the tertön would take a terma out in the presence of more than one thousand people: thus there was no basis for doubt. As the rock opened and the interior became visible, we saw it was filled with scintillating rainbow light. The terma articles were hot to the touch. Once there was an immense amount of *sindhura* powder, so much that it poured out. Chokgyur Lingpa often brought brocade cloth along to place the precious articles upon. Many of them got burn marks because the termas were so hot. No one other than him could hold them." I later saw some of these scorched pieces of brocade, red and yellow in color, in Chokgyur Lingpa's *tengam* [room of sacred objects].

My grandmother continued, "Chokgyur Lingpa would then place the terma — sometimes it would be a statue — to cool off atop the brocade on an open shrine. He explained to those present how the terma was concealed, why it was revealed now, the benefits of receiving its blessings, and so forth. The assembly of more than one thousand people wept out of faith and devotion, the air humming with crying. Even if you were a stubborn intellectual, all skepticism would melt away. Everyone was struck with wonder."

It had to be this way, because Tibetans, especially those in the Eastern Tibetan province of Kham, were known to be extremely skeptical. They didn't automatically believe a tertön. But Chokgyur Lingpa was beyond doubt and dispute, because he repeatedly revealed termas with innumerable witnesses present.

Terma teachings, being the direct words of Padmasambhava, are, when revealed at their destined time, of a profundity that is hard to match by any other treatise. They possess unique blessings — but the blessings depend upon your trust and devotion. Karsey Kongtrül, the son of the 15th Karmapa, once told me, "Three times I performed the drubchen ceremony of the *Tukdrub Barchey Künsel* terma of Chokgyur Lingpa, and each time wonderful signs of accomplishment appeared." "Please tell me what they were," I asked. "Once a profuse amount of nectar poured forth, very sweet and slightly sour like excellent chang, from the torma on the shrine and flowed all the way to the entrance of the temple. Another time, the *amrita* and *rakta* on the shrine began to boil, sounding like boiling water. The third time we also prepared sacred medicine, and its sweet fragrance could be smelled seven days walk away. In my whole life I have never witnessed signs as amazing as during those three times." This could also be due to the combination of the profound terma teaching and such an extremely great master. There are many other stories of nectar pouring forth from the shrine torma during drubchen ceremonies at Chokgyur Lingpa's Tsikey Monastery.

The great master Jamyang Khyentse Wangpo also revealed a terma identical to *Tukdrub Barchey Künsel*. After meeting Chokgyur Lingpa and carefully examining and comparing the two versions of this terma teaching, Jamyang Khyentse Wangpo burned his own, saying, "Since the words and the meaning are identical, what is the use of having two! Yours, being an earth terma, is more profound and will be more effectual than my mind terma." Thus the blessings of two lineages, earth and mind terma, were fused into a single stream. An earth terma is material and taken out from the earth while mind terma is revealed out of the expanse of realization. It is said that earth termas bring greater benefit to beings because they often contain yellow parchment with symbolic script hidden by Padmasambhava.

This symbolic script called dakini letters is incredibly profound. To quote a tantric scripture: "Treasure letters are the body of magical emanation. They are also speech to understand sounds and words. By realizing their meaning, they are also mind." In this way, enlightened body, speech and mind are all contained within the letters of dakini script. This script is itself nirmanakaya, the body of magical creation. For a master to give a reading transmission of even a short chant the physical script is always necessary — it is not permissible to repeat from memory. Similarly, there is a profound difference between having or not having the yellow parchment with the dakini script present.

The instructions of Padmasambhava often conclude with his command to his direct disciples not to propagate them immediately but to conceal them for the benefit of future followers. The reason was to preserve the continuity of pith instructions. Without concealing the direct advice as terma treasures, their lineage could have died out over the many centuries. Teachings do disappear, even though their initial propagator could fly through the sky and traverse solid matter. Take for instance the great siddha Karma Pakshi; his writings filled about one hundred volumes, but today we have only three of them left. That's how it goes. The female master Machig Labdrön's instructions on *Chö* practice, cutting through ego-clinging, exceeded 80 or 90 volumes, but where do you find all these precious teachings today?

Within the Nyingma lineage, none of the great masters are more renowned for learnedness than Rongzompa and Longchenpa. Even though Rongzompa is generally considered to be more learned, Longchenpa excelled in his teachings on the view. Each of the them had a collection of writings of more than 60 or 70 volumes; but today they are not found anywhere. Teachings do disappear!

Terma teachings, on the other hand, are inexhaustible. When an authentic tertön has a vision of the symbolic script, each syllable becomes an entire magical city. Moreover, the letters of the teaching to be written down remain in midair until they have been copied correctly; if a sentence lingers on, it's because the tertön made a spelling mistake. This is how the correctness of the decoding is ensured.

We can easily agree on the preciousness of Padmasambhava and Yeshe Tsogyal. The teachings they concealed in lakes and in solid rock do not go to waste. As soon as the right time has come, the writing appears vividly and distinctly within the tertön's field of experience. Prior to the actual discovery of a terma, the tertön will receive the guidance scripture, a short text explaining its location, the inventory of teachings, and its correct time of revelation. When going to that place, my grandmother said, "Chokgyur Lingpa was guided by a beam of light from his heart to the terma, leading him directly to the place of concealment."

Padmasambhava could see the three times of past, present and future as clearly as an object placed in the palm of our hand, so most definitely he could also see what type of teaching would be appropriate for people of future generations. When he scolds his chief disciple Yeshe Tsogyal or Tibetans in general, no matter which country you happen to have been born in, you should feel free to take his criticism personally so as to remove hidden faults. Doubt prevents benefit; don't be like a cave facing north where the sun never reaches. When Padmasambhava points out what constitutes a fault and what obstructs the path of enlightenment, such truths are valid, not only for Tibetans, but for everyone who sincerely wants to follow a spiritual practice. Since we live in an era different from that of the eighth century, you can feel free to exchange the word 'Tibetans' with 'people of this world.'

Yeshe Tsogyal was the chief compiler of Padmasambhava's words, and without her we would not have so many of his teachings. Ananda was the chief compiler of Buddha Shakyamuni's words in terms of the sutra teachings, while Vajrapani compiled his tantric instructions; in essence they were identical. Yeshe Tsogyal had what is called 'unforgetting recall;' she never forgot a single sentence she heard. Isn't it quite useless to hear something and forget it completely?

This compiler of Padmasambhava's teachings was herself an emanation of the female buddhas Prajnaparamita, Vajra Varahi, and Arya Tara. She appeared in our world for this specific purpose; it was her special mandate. Ananda, Vajrapani, and Yeshe Tsogyal are all described as having perfect recall, the power of remembrance that never forgets. This unforgetting recall is the same as what we call nondistraction, because forgetting and being distracted are of an identical nature. In this book we have the teachings she heard, never forgot, codified, and finally concealed as terma treasures for us. Yeshe Tsogyal was a woman: there may be some people who believe that only men can attain enlightenment, but her life is proof of the opposite. In actual fact, the awakened state of mind is neither male nor female.

The style of prose in *Advice from the Lotus-Born*, the form of questions and answers between Padmasambhava and Yeshe Tsogyal and other of his close disciples, is identical to that found in most sutras and tantras, especially in their opening chapter, called the 'setting.' You find that most of the Vinaya scriptures on monastic discipline came about because the Buddha was asked how to deal with six incorrigible followers who would perform any type of wrongdoing. After being presented with the story of their latest adventure, the Buddha would set down a new rule of what should be prohibited for a monk.

Another point is that you hardly find a single sutra discourse that wasn't given in response to someone's question. First a person would ask the Buddha about some topic, and the teaching would be given. Similarly with this type of oral instruction, it is given only in reply to a request. The tantras were expounded in a similar fashion: the central figure of the mandala would emanate a surrounding retinue, the members of which would then request the tantric teachings. In short, the question-and-answer format is the traditional style.

There is a prophecy that the "teachings of the Buddha will spread further and further north". Nepal is to the north of India, and after that, isn't Tibet to the north of Nepal? "Later on, they will return to the central land and then go west." I'm not sure where these words are from; they may be from a terma of Padmasambhava or maybe they were spoken by the Buddha himself. But most certainly the prophecy exists; I heard it from Dzongsar Khyentse Rinpoche. "From now on the Buddhadharma will spread further west," he said.

On another note, since both Buddha Shakyamuni and Padmasambhava appear in one billion forms in each of the one billion world systems, is there any reason why their emanations haven't appeared in all the countries of this world? Who can state with certainty that a single place exists where a buddha's blessings have not reached? Of course we rely on history books to tell us where and when Buddhism spread, but I feel that the Buddha's activity is all-pervasive, encompassing our entire world.

For instance, I was often told that Padmasambhava visited every place throughout Tibet and Kham, blessing every mountain, cave and lake, and not leaving out any place, even as small as a horse's hoof print. So why would he have left out any other place in this world?

All teachings by the Buddha are of course true, but they differ in the degree to which emphasis is placed on the relative or ultimate meaning. Each is important, in the sense that the relative level guides by means of teachings on correct conduct, while the ultimate works through instructions on the correct view. These teachings can be given in the form of pith advice or concise oral instructions.

It is generally known that one should 'descend with the view' from above while 'ascending with the conduct from below.' To descend with the view from above refers to recognizing the outlook of the Great Perfection, while to ascend with the conduct means to practice in accordance with the eight lower vehicles. In the Vajrayana context, this refers especially to training in the ten topics of tantra.

To conclude, the various collections of Padmasambhava's advice contain instructions on both view and conduct. It is my opinion that one should present teachings exactly in their original form, without adding anything and without leaving anything out. If, for instance, you leave out the instructions on the view and present only his teachings on conduct, Padmasambhava's words become incomplete. In the ultimate intent of the view, you definitely hear statements such as "There is no karma, no good and no evil." But please understand the statements in their correct context!

Without the view, all teachings become only expedient, superficial instructions on behavior. If you lose the view in the conduct, there is never any opportunity for liberation; but if you lose the conduct in the view, you stray into believing that there is neither good nor evil, that both are empty. To understand Vajrayana, we must learn how the tantric teachings are concealed within the six limits and four modes.

The expedient meaning focuses on conduct, while the definitive meaning involves the view. As Milarepa said, "Fooling yourself with the expedient meaning, you lose the opportunity to realize the true meaning."

Spoken by Tulku Urgyen Rinpoche
Asura Cave Temple, October 1993

ADVICE
FROM THE
LOTUS-BORN

❧

THE JEWEL SPIKE TESTAMENT:

ঞ৶৸

THIS ADVICE WAS SPOKEN TO YESHE TSOGYAL

I, the Lotus-Born master of Uddiyana,
Trained in the Dharma for the welfare of myself and others.
To the east of the Vajra Seat
I studied and became learned in the Sutra teachings.

To the south, west and north
I studied the collections of Vinaya, Abhidharma,
And the Paramita teachings.

In Bhasudhara I studied Kriya.
In the land of Uddiyana I studied Yoga.
In the country of Zahor I studied the two sections of Tantra.

In the land of Jah I studied Kilaya.
In the country of Singha I studied Hayagriva.
In the land of Marutsey I studied Mamo.
In Nepal I studied Yamantaka.
At the Vajra Seat I studied Amrita.

The four sections of Father Tantra and Mother Tantra,
Including the Guhyasamaja,
I studied to erudition in the land of Jala.
The Great Perfection I learned from my naturally aware mind.
I have realized that all phenomena are like dreams, like magic.

In the land of Tibet I performed immense actions for the welfare of
    beings.
In the age of degeneration I will benefit beings.
Therefore I concealed innumerable terma treasures
Which will meet with destined people.

All you fortunate ones who connect with these termas,
Fulfill the command of the Lotus-Born!

Thus he spoke.

Emaho! At the end of this age my terma treasures will flourish in this snowy
land of Tibet. Listen here, all of you who will follow my advice at that time!

It is difficult to realize the nature of Ati Yoga of the Great Perfection, so
train in it! This nature is the awakened state of mind. Although your body remains human, your mind arrives at the stage of buddhahood.

No matter how profound, how vast, or how all-encompassing the teachings
of the Great Perfection may be, they are all included within this: Don't meditate
on or fabricate even as much as an atom and don't be distracted for even as
much as an instant.[1]

There is a danger that people who fail to comprehend this will use this
platitude: "It is all right not to meditate!" Their minds remain fettered by the
distractions of samsaric business, although when someone realizes the nature of
nonmeditation, they should have liberated samsara and nirvana into equality.
When realization occurs you should definitely be free from samsara, so that your
disturbing emotions naturally subside and become original wakefulness. What is
the use of a realization that fails to reduce your disturbing emotions?

However, some people will indulge in the five poisons while refraining
from meditation. They have not realized the true nature and will surely go to
hell.

Don't profess a view you haven't realized! Since the view is devoid of viewing, mind essence is an expanse of great emptiness. Since the meditation is without meditating, leave your individual experience free from fixation. Since the conduct is without acting, it is unfabricated naturalness. Since the fruition is without abandoning or achieving, it is the dharmakaya of great bliss. These four sentences are words from my heart. Contradict them and you fail to discover the nature of Ati Yoga.

At the end of the future age, there will be many perverted practitioners who will treat the Dharma as merchandise. At that time, all of you who obey my words, do not forsake the ten spiritual activities.

Although your realization is equal to that of the buddhas', make offerings to the Three Jewels. Although you have gained mastery over your mind, direct your innermost aims towards the Dharma. Although the nature of the Great Perfection is supreme, don't disparage other teachings.

Although you have realized that buddhas and sentient beings are equal, embrace all beings with compassion. Although the paths and bhumis are beyond training and journeying, don't forsake purifying your obscurations through Dharma activities. Although the accumulations are beyond gathering, don't sever the roots of conditioned virtue.

Although your mind lies beyond birth and death, this illusory body does die, so practice while remembering death. Although you experience dharmata free from thought, maintain the attitude of bodhichitta. Although you have attained the fruition of dharmakaya, keep company with your yidam deity.

Although dharmakaya is not some other place, seek the true meaning. Although buddhahood is not anywhere else, dedicate any virtue you create towards unexcelled enlightenment. Although everything experienced is original wakefulness, don't let your mind stray into samsara.

Although your mind essence is the awakened one, always worship the deity and your master. Although you have realized the nature of the Great Perfection, don't abandon your yidam deity. Those who, instead of doing this, speak foolishly with boastful words only damage the Three Jewels and will find not even an instant of happiness.

The guru said: Human beings don't think of death. A man's life is like a pile of chaff or a feather on a mountain pass. The demon Lord of Death comes suddenly, like an avalanche or a storm. Disturbing emotions are like straw catching fire. Your life-span decreases like the shadows of the setting sun.

All sentient beings of the three realms entangle themselves in their self-created black snake of anger. They pierce themselves with the horns of their self-created red ox of desire. They obscure themselves with their self-produced dense darkness of dullness. They chain themselves to their self-created cliff of conceit. They mangle themselves with their self-created jackal of envy. People don't notice that they fail to escape the five dangerous defiles of disturbing emotions. They do anything to experience the samsaric pleasures of just this life.

This life is crossed in a brief moment, but samsara is endless. What will you do in the next life? Also, the length of this life is not guaranteed: the time of death lies uncertain, and like a convict taken to the scaffold, you draw closer to death with each step.

All beings are impermanent and die. Haven't you heard about the people who died in the past? Haven't you seen any of your relatives die? Don't you notice that we grow old? And still, rather than practicing the Dharma, you forget about past grief. Rather than dreading future misery, you ignore the suffering of the lower realms.

Chased by temporary circumstances, tied by the rope of dualistic fixation, exhausted by the river of desire, caught in the web of samsaric existence, held captive by the tight shackles of karmic ripening — even when the tidings of the Dharma reach you, you still cling to diversions and remain careless. Is it that death doesn't happen to people like you? I pity all sentient beings who think in this way!

The guru said: When you keep in mind the misery of dying, it becomes clear that all activities are causes for suffering, so give them up. Cut all ties, even the smallest, and meditate in solitude on the remedy of emptiness. Nothing whatsoever will help you at the time of death, so practice the Dharma since it is your best companion.

Your master and the Three Jewels are the best escort, so earnestly take refuge. To practice the Dharma is what helps your state of mind the most. Remember what you have heard, since the Dharma is the most trustworthy.

No matter which teaching you practice, give up feeling sleepy, lethargic and lazy. Instead, don the armor of diligence. No matter which teaching you have comprehended, don't separate yourself from its meaning.

Padmasambhava said: Do like this if you want to practice the true Dharma! Keep your master's oral instructions in mind. Don't conceptualize your experience, as it just makes you attached or angry. Day and night, look into your mind. If your stream of mind contains any nonvirtue, renounce it from the core of your heart and pursue virtue.

Moreover, when you see other people committing evil, feel compassion for them. It is entirely possible that you will feel attachment to or aversion for certain sense objects. Give that up. When you feel attachment towards something attractive or aversion towards something repulsive, understand that to be your mind's delusion, nothing but a magical illusion.

When you hear pleasant or unpleasant words, understand them to be an empty resounding, like an echo. When you encounter severe misfortune and misery, understand it to be a temporary occurrence, a deluded experience. Recognize that the innate nature is never apart from you.

To obtain a human body is extremely difficult, so it is foolish to ignore the Dharma once having found it. Only the Dharma can help you; everything else is worldly beguilement.

Again the guru said: Beings with inferior karma aim at the grandeur and vanity of this world and act with no thought of karmic ripening. Future misery will endure much longer than that of the present, so feel motherly love and compassion for the beings of the three realms. Keep constant company with the awakened mind of bodhichitta. Forsake the ten nonvirtues and adopt the ten virtues.

Don't regard any sentient being as your enemy: to do so is only your mind's delusion. Don't seek food and drink through lies and deceit. Though your belly will be full in this life, it will weigh heavy in the following.

Don't get involved in business and making profits: in general, it is distracting for both yourself and others. Attach no importance to wealth, because it is the enemy of meditation and Dharma practice.

Dwelling only on food is a cause of distraction: keep your meditation provisions sufficient merely to sustain yourself. Don't live in villages or areas which promote attachment and aversion. When your body is in seclusion your mind will be also. Give up idle gossip and speak less. If you hurt another's feelings, both of you create negative karma.

In general, all sentient beings without exception have been your parents, so don't allow yourself to feel attached or hostile. Maintain a peaceful frame of mind. Give up angry and harsh words; instead speak with a smiling face.

Your parents' kindness cannot be repaid even if you sacrifice your life, so be respectful in thought, word, and deed. Virtue and evil both come from perceived objects and companions, so don't keep company with evildoers. Don't remain in a place where people are hostile towards you and which furthers anger and desire. If you do, it only increases disturbing emotions in yourself and others.

Stay where your state of mind is at ease and your Dharma practice will automatically progress. To remain in places of extreme attachment and aversion is only distracting. Stay where your Dharma practice develops.

If you become conceited, your virtues diminish, so give up being arrogant and haughty. If you become disappointed and disheartened, console yourself and be your own counsel. Re-embark on the path.

The guru said: If you want to genuinely practice the Dharma, do what is virtuous, even the most minute deed. Renounce what is evil, even the tiniest deed. The largest ocean is made from drops of water; even Mount Sumeru and the four continents are made of tiny atoms.

It doesn't matter whether your act of giving is as small as a single sesame seed; if you give with compassion and bodhichitta you achieve hundredfold merit. If you give without the bodhichitta resolve, your merit will not increase even if you give away horses and cattle.

Don't indulge in flattery and half-hearted friendships. Remain honest in thought and deed. The foremost Dharma practice is to keep honesty in thought and deed. The foundation of Dharma practice rests on pure samaya, compassion and bodhichitta. The samayas of Secret Mantra, the bodhisattva precepts, and the rules of the shravakas are all included within this.

The guru said: Spend all your food supplies and wealth on virtuous deeds. Some people say, "One needs wealth at the time of death." But when you are struck by a fatal sickness, you cannot apportion your pain out for money, no matter how many helpers you have, and your pain is no greater if you have none.

At that time it makes no difference whether you have helpers, servants, attendants and wealth. All are all causes for attachment. Attachment binds you, even attachment to your deity and to the Dharma. The rich person's attachment to his thousand ounces of gold and the poor man's attachment to his needle and thread are equally binding. Give up the attachment that blocks the door to liberation.

When you die, it is the same whether your body is cremated on a pyre of sandalwood or consumed by birds and dogs in an unpeopled place. You go on, accompanied by whatever good or evil deeds you committed while alive. Your bad name or good reputation, your stock of food and wealth, and all your helpers and servants are left behind.

On the day you die you will need a sublime master, so seek one out [beforehand]. Without a master you cannot possibly awaken to enlightenment, so follow a qualified master and accomplish whatever he commands.

Again the guru said: Listen here, fortunate people of future times who follow the words of Padmakara! First of all, when embarking on the path you must be diligent. For so long in the past, you were engrossed in deluded experience; for incalculable aeons, anything you did went astray in delusion. Cut through this delusion right now while you have obtained a human body.

All sentient beings are obscured by the darkness of the ignorant all-ground. When dualistic experience arose, it was solidified through dualistic fixation. No matter what sentient beings do, they commit miserable deeds. This prison of delusion of the six classes of beings is so tight!

It is extremely difficult to obtain a human body. Having obtained it, only a few people hear the name of the Buddha. After hearing it, it is extremely rare that someone feels faith. And even feeling faith once, after entering the Dharma many people like stubborn beasts break their samayas and precepts and head downhill. Seeing these sentient beings, the bodhisattvas despair, and I, Padmakara, grieve.

Tsogyal, in a place where the teachings of the Buddha are present, even people who obtained a perfect human body have since innumerable lifetimes gathered boundless merit, but they still possess the complete karma of the six classes of beings.

Some of them, upon hearing of the qualities of the Buddha, are set ablaze with attachment and anger, worried that other people will be interested too. Having joined the followers of the Buddha's teachings, they worry that samsara will be depleted. This type of attachment and anger is the seed for the hell realms. In future lives such people take rebirth in places where they never hear the name of the Three Jewels.

You people who live now or appear in the future and who correctly listen to the words of Padmakara, this is what you should do: In order to take advantage of the human body you have obtained, you need the sublime Dharma. People who cling to and yearn for mundane prestige and fame rather than practicing the Dharma belong to the highest level among animals.

If you doubt this, then ponder carefully: to be anxious that this body is comfortable, to be anxious that it will last, to be anxious that one triumphs, to be anxious that one's intimates are benefited, to be anxious that one's hated enemies are repaid in kind — all these are something that worldly people possess. The birds in the sky, the mice on the earth, the ants who live under stones and rocks all have the same as well. All sentient beings have it.

To have less harmful enemies than other beings is merely the highest level among the animals. In order to practice the Dharma you must cast away attachment to a country. Your homeland is the birthplace of attachment and anger.

Keep as much food and wealth as convenient to take and carry. Do so until you have cast away attachment to food and clothing. Don't keep possessions that become a distraction. Seek a place unfrequented by savage people. Keeping to food that is sufficient to simply sustain you, live in solitude free from companionship.

At first, purify your misdeeds. Next, look into your mind! The fact that the natural state of mind doesn't last but projects thoughts is proof that it is empty. The uninterrupted occurrence of projecting thoughts is its cognizant clarity. Don't pursue the projection of thoughts. Don't cling to the cognizant clarity. By relaxing your attention and recognizing its essence, your natural awareness dawns as dharmakaya.

At times, do the practices for clearing hindrances and bringing forth enhancement. If you can follow my testament in this way, you will attain the state of Vajradhara in this very lifetime.

Tsogyal, someone with a dark brown and wrathful form will appear near the end of the teachings of Shakyamuni. For his sake, conceal these words of mine within a casket of brown rhino skin.

Thus he spoke.

The testament of the Lotus-Born master of Uddiyana entitled the Jewel Spike is hereby completed.

This was revealed by Rigdzin Gödem, the Vidyadhara with the Vulture Feather, from the white treasure-trove to the east.

Samaya, seal, seal.

May it be virtuous.

May it be virtuous.

May it be virtuous.

SARVA MANGALAM.

ADVICE TO TRISONG DEUTSEN:

꧁

EMAHO! THE MASTER PADMASAMBHAVA was invited by King Trisong Deutsen to tame the construction site and build Samye, the Glorious Spontaneously Perfected Fulfillment of Boundless Wishes. Later, when conducting the
consecration, the king invited the master who was dressed in a dark maroon
cloak of brocade to sit upon a throne of silken cushions in the upper central
chamber. He served the master wine made from rice, and placed full goblets of
both gold and silver at his right and left hands. The king offered a variety of material objects and arranged upon a golden mandala plate the size of one cubit
flowers of turquoise in the manner of the seven precious articles. From his own
neck he took a turquoise ornament known as Radiant Maru and placed it as the
representation of the sun, and another known as Kenru Kongchok as a representation of the moon. He assembled additional precious articles on the golden
plate to represent Mount Sumeru and the four continents, and offered it to the
master with these words of praise:

> Without depending upon a mother and father, your nirmanakaya form
> appeared from within a lotus flower,
> It abides to influence beings as the vajra body that cuts the stream of
> birth and death.

From the unconfined expanse of realization, you reveal the buddha mind
    to worthy people.
Skilled in influencing with a variety of means, you bind the haughty gods
    and demons under oath.
With the perfect activity of the three kayas, your nirmanakaya form
    exceeds that of all other buddhas.
I bow to the lotus form of Vajra Tötreng and praise you with devotion.

Although you do not possess clinging or attachment when enjoying the
    five sense pleasures,
You compassionately accept them so that all beings can create merit.
Please consider me kindly as I supplicate you to bestow the supreme,
    profound meaning!

    The master responded, "Your Majesty! Are you fond of my present form?"
"Yes, I am," the king replied, and continued:

Free from diseases of the four elements, beyond both birth and death,
You possess the eminent compassion to act for the welfare of beings,
Your mind forever abides as the innate nature of dharmata;
Yes, I am fond of your form, the protector of beings!

    The master then said:

You should know that one's master is more important
Than even the thousand buddhas of this aeon.
Why is that? It is because all the buddhas of this aeon
Appeared after having followed a master.
Before there was a master
The word 'buddhas' never existed.

    It is also said:

The master is the buddha, the master is the Dharma,
In the same way the master is also the sangha;
He is thus the root of the Three Jewels.
Setting aside all other worship,
Endeavor to serve your master.
By pleasing him, you will receive all the attainments you desire.

The king then inquired of Padmasambhava: Great master, when trying to accomplish the effect, buddhahood, from the cause, a sentient being, first of all the view of realization is of exclusive importance. What is meant by 'possessing the view of realization'?

The master replied: The pinnacle of all views is the bodhichitta essence of awakened mind. All of the great billionfold universes, all the sugatas of the ten directions, and all of the beings of the three realms are of one nature in that they that are included within the bodhichitta essence of awakened mind. 'Mind' here means the diversity that arises from the unmade.

Well, you may then ask, 'What is the difference between buddhas and sentient beings?' It is nothing other than realizing or not realizing mind. The substance of the awakened state, of buddha, is present within you, but you don't recognize it. Not recognizing their minds, beings stray into the six streams of existence. You may then ask, 'What is the way to realize mind?' For that, it is taught, you need the oral instructions of a master.

In this regard, 'mind' is that which thinks and cognizes; there is indeed something that experiences. Don't seek this mind outside, look within! Let mind search for itself! Reach certainty about how the nature of mind is!

At first, from where does mind arise? Right now, where does it stay? At the end, look into where it goes! When your mind looks into itself, it finds no place from where it arises, remains, or goes to. There is no explanation of 'this is how it is.' 'Mind' is discovered to be without something outside or inside. It does not have someone that looks; it is not the act of looking. It is experienced as a great original wakefulness without center or edge, an immense all-pervasiveness that is primordially empty and free. This original wakefulness is intrinsic and self-existing. It is not made right now, but is present within yourself from the very beginning. Decide firmly that the view is to recognize just that!

To 'possess confidence' in this means to realize that like space, mind is spontaneously present from the beginning. Like the sun, it is free from any basis for the darkness of ignorance. Like a lotus flower, it is untainted by faults. Like gold, it doesn't alter its own nature. Like the ocean, it is unmoving. Like a river, it is unceasing. Like Mount Sumeru, it is utterly unchanging. Once you realize that this is how it is [and stabilize it], that is called 'possessing the view of realization.'

The king asked: What is meant by 'possessing the experience of meditation'?

The master replied: Listen here, Your Majesty! To 'possess the experience of meditation' means to leave your mind uncontrived, uncorrupted and fresh. Let your mind rest in its natural, unrestrained and free state. By neither placing your mind on something outside nor concentrating inwardly, you remain free of focus. Within this great equal state of your innate nature, let your mind stay unmoved, just like the flame of a butter lamp that is not moved by the wind.

Within this state, experiences can occur: your consciousness may become overflowing, bright or stop altogether; blissful, radiant or free of thoughts; it may feel murky, without reference point, and out of tune with the ways of this world. If these experiences occur, don't attach any special importance to them, as they are just temporary experiences. Don't cling to or fixate on them at all! That is called 'possessing the experience of meditation.'

The king asked: What is meant by 'possessing the equal taste of conduct'?

The master replied: 'Conduct' here means to be uninterrupted in meditation; without being distracted, even though there is no thing being meditated upon. Like the ceaseless flow of a river, you remember throughout all situations, whether walking, moving about, lying down or sitting. 'Equal taste' means to embrace whatever you see, or whichever of the five sense pleasures occur, with the recognition of your innate nature, free from attachment or clinging. You do not accept or reject anything at all, just like the analogy of arriving on an island of precious gold. This is called 'possessing the equal taste of conduct.'

Again the king asked: What makes one 'cross the dangerous defile of moving thoughts'?

The master answered: When conceptual thinking occurs while resting in meditation, whatever arises does so out of your own mind. Since mind does not consist of any concrete essence whatsoever, thinking is itself empty of any real entity. Like the analogy of a cloud that appears within space and vanishes again into space, thinking occurs within mind and dissolves again into mind. In nature, conceptual thinking is the innate dharmata.

'Crossing the dangerous defile' means that when mind moves into a variety of thoughts, you should direct your attention into this mind itself. Like a thief entering an empty house, empty thoughts cannot in any way harm an empty mind. That is called having 'crossed the dangerous defile of moving thoughts.'

The king asked the master: How does one 'gain the unchanging confidence of fruition'?

The master replied: Listen to this, Your Majesty! The awakened mind of bodhichitta is not created through causes nor destroyed through circumstances. It is not made by ingenious buddhas nor manufactured by clever sentient beings. It is originally present in you as your natural possession. When you recognize it through your master's oral instructions, since mind is the forefather of the buddhas, it is like the analogy of recognizing someone you already know.

All the buddhas of the three times awaken to enlightenment in the continuity of actualizing this after attaining stability, just like the analogy of a prince ascending to the throne. To awaken to what is spontaneously present from the beginning, free from fear and intimidation, is called 'possessing the confidence of fruition.'

The king asked the master: What makes you 'cut through the limitations of sidetracks and faults'?

The master responded: Your Majesty, to feel either hope or fear is due to the fault of not realizing the view. The awakened bodhichitta mind of awareness neither hopes to get enlightened nor fears falling to the state of sentient beings.

To hold the concepts of meditator and meditation object is due to the fault of not cutting through the projections of dualistic mind. Your innate nature of dharmata, free of constructs, does not have an object to be meditated upon, 'someone' who meditates, or any meditation to be cultivated whatsoever.

To accept or reject is due to the fault of not cutting through attachment and fixation. The originally free and empty nature of mind has neither something to be accomplished to which you can cling, nor something to be rejected to which you can be hostile. It has neither virtues that must be accepted nor evils that must be rejected.

To be attached to possessions is due to the fault of not understanding how to practice. Practice in regards to any thing is to be free from focus and fixation, and to understand that attachment and clinging are devoid of ground and root.

To condense all of this into a single sentence: the view is to be free from convictions,[2] meditation is to not place [the mind on] anything, experience is to be free from savoring the taste, and fruition is beyond attainment. The buddhas of the three times have not taught, are not teaching, and will not teach it to be any other than this! That is called 'cutting through the limitations of sidetracks and faults.'

The king asked the master: What does it mean to 'clear away the fault of conviction'?

The master replied: Even though you have realized that your mind is the buddha, don't forsake your master! Even though you have realized appearances to be mind, don't interrupt conditioned roots of virtue! Even though you don't hope for buddhahood, honor the sublime Three Jewels! Even though you don't fear samsara, avoid even the minutest misdeed! Even though you have gained the unchanging confidence of your innate nature, don't belittle any spiritual teaching! Even though you experience the qualities of samadhi, higher perceptions and the like, give up conceit and pretentiousness! Even though you have realized that samsara and nirvana are nondual, don't cease to have compassion for sentient beings!

Again the king asked: What does it mean to 'gain certainty'?

The master responded: Gain certainty in the fact that since the very beginning your own mind is the awakened state of buddhahood. Gain certainty in the fact that all phenomena are the magical display of your mind. Gain certainty in the fact that the fruition is present in yourself and is not to be sought elsewhere. Gain certainty in the fact that your master is the buddha in person. Gain certainty in the fact that the nature of view and meditation is the realization of the buddhas. To gain such confidence you must practice![3]

Again the king asked: What does it mean to 'possess the transmission of oral instructions'?

The master replied: By means of blessings Samantabhadra expounded these secret words into the ears of Vajrasattva. Vajrasattva poured them into the locket of Garab Dorje's ears. Garab Dorje entrusted them to the center of Shri Singha's heart. Shri Singha bestowed them upon me, Padmasambhava. Trisong Deutsen, keep them in the core of your heart![4]

The master instructed the king: Your Majesty, unless you realize the non-arising nature of dharmata, even though you have been born in the body of a monarch, life passes like a bubble in the water.

Unless you experience the innate nature of dharmata beyond thought, [you will suffer when] your kingdom and worldly power, which are as insubstantial as a rainbow, fade and vanish.

Unless you keep company with your friend, self-existing awareness, when you leave this life you will [not be able to cut your attachment] to your queens, servants and subjects, [who are no more than] acquaintances left behind on a journey.

Unless you grow accustomed to the natural state of view and meditation, you will circle from one life to the next, like on the rim of a waterwheel, entering at birth and exiting at death.

Unless you rule your kingdom with the truth of peace, strict laws are like a poisonous tree that will destroy itself. Great king, I beg you to rule in accord with the Dharma!

Again the master instructed the king: Your Majesty, at the end of this age people with hanker after excellent teachings, but will not realize them. Not following the word of the Dharma, many will profess to be practitioners. At that time there will be plenty of braggarts but few accomplished people. When the Buddhadharma ceases in China, Tibet and Mongolia, like a coat of mail being broken, people will be hard to tame. At that time these teachings must protect the Buddhadharma, so you must conceal them as a terma treasure.

Your Majesty, in your last life you will meet with these teachings and those who protect the Buddhadharma. You will then stop the stream of rebirth and proceed to the stage of a vidyadhara, so don't publicize them now!

Becoming overjoyed, the king presented a mandala offering of gold and made countless prostrations and circumambulations.

Seal of treasure.
Seal of concealment.
Seal of entrustment.

No Conflict Between the Lesser and Greater Vehicles:

∾✦∾

KING TRISONG DEUTSEN OFFERED A MANDALA of gold to the great master Padmakara and said: How amazing! Great master, I beg you to teach the method of practice that shows that there is no conflict between the lesser and the greater vehicles.

The master replied: Emaho, great king, it is rare to repeatedly be born as a king in a perfect human body endowed with merit, so it is important to govern the kingdom of Dharma.

You may keep a strict rule regarding mundane activities but it brings harm to all beings, so it is important to train in bodhichitta.

You may cherish this illusory body with great fondness, but the time of death lies uncertain. Your white hairs and wrinkles are omens of death, so it is important to feel weariness and exert yourself in the remedies, the practice of Dharma.

The cause for entering the path of liberation is to keep a sense of shame and modesty, shunning misdeeds, so it is important to observe the vows and precepts without impairing them.

Sentient beings are the object of compassion, so be free from prejudice towards new acquaintances. It is important to bring all of your retinue, subjects and relatives to the Dharma and to support them.

One can never accumulate enough things such as food and wealth, so it is important to use them for the sake of the Dharma without letting them be wasted by becoming food for enemies and ghosts.

Without faith and devotion one does not receive the essence of the oral instructions, so it is important to honor and serve the lineage masters with faith, devotion and trust.

It is the master who shows you the wisdom of buddhahood present within yourself, so it is important to request the oral instructions from a master endowed with the hearing lineage and then put them into practice.

You don't receive the blessings when you let your body, speech and mind remain ordinary, so it is important to concentrate your body, speech and mind on being deity, mantra and the innate state beyond concepts.

If you pursue ordinary deeds your body, speech and mind will run wild in worldly experience, so it is important to skillfully give up bad company and keep to mountain retreats.

Your parents, brothers, sons and consorts are all like passing travelers. You will not remain together, so it is important to give up attachment and refrain from female company, the root of samsara.

All the achievements, honor and fame of this life are the cause for distraction and obstacles, so it is important to give up preoccupation with this life and completely renounce the eight worldly concerns.

All your present experiences, the manifold feelings of pleasure and pain, are superficial and unreal, so it is important to recognize that all that appears and exists is devoid of independent existence, just like a magical apparition or a dream.

The mind is like an untamed horse running wild wherever it pleases, so it is important to always place mindfulness and conscientiousness on guard.

The nature of your mind, which cannot be pinpointed, is itself innate, self-existing and original wakefulness; it is important to look into yourself and recognize your nature.

When grasping hold of the mind it does not remain, so it is important to relax body and mind from within while leaving the attention in its natural state.

All tampering and fabrication is your thoughts' double delusion, so it is important to relax rampant thought activity while letting it be liberated in its natural state.

All effort and attempts to accomplish are tied by the rope of ambition, so it is important to allow [your thinking] to be cleared in itself, free from effort and ambition.

You do not attain buddhahood while harboring hope or fear, so it is important to resolve that the empty and nonarising nature of mind is beyond a buddhahood to be attained or a samsara to fall into.

Emaho, listen, king! If you practice like this you will not have any conflict between the greater or lesser vehicles, between Mantra or the Philosophical vehicles, or the causal and resultant vehicles, so, great king, keep that in mind.

At the end of this age, great king, you will cut the stream of rebirth and bring samsara to an end. The original wakefulness of buddhahood will dawn within you and you will unceasingly accomplish the welfare of beings. Conceal these teachings as precious treasures!

Hearing this advice on the union of development and completion, the king was overjoyed and made numerous prostrations and circumambulations and scattered gold dust.

This was the oral instruction on important advice that contradicts none of the general vehicles.

Seal of treasure.
Seal of concealment.
Seal of entrustment.

THE GOLDEN ROSARY OF NECTAR:

꧁

HOMAGE TO THE GREAT MASTER PADMASAMBHAVA! The one known as the Lotus-Born of Uddiyana is the emanation body of all the buddhas of the three times, the great vidyadhara of indestructible omniscience. He was invited to Tibet by the lord and ruler [Trisong Deutsen]. While residing there, I, Tsogyal, served him as consort and attendant. Once, when staying in the Tidro Cave at Shotö, I was pointed out and recognized the meaning of the *Innermost, Unexcelled Heart Essence of the Great Perfection.* I resolved the natural state through the view as direct experience, without leaving it as an assumption. Struck with wonder, I, the princess of Kharchen, asked:

Amazing! Great master, since all the key points of the *Heart Essence of Secret Mantra* are contained within the three principles of essence, nature and capacity, do these three have any deviations or not?

The master said: Tsogyal, it is excellent that you ask this. All the key points of the *Innermost Heart Essence* are indeed contained within essence, nature and capacity. When a person doesn't understand there are ways of going astray. To explain this, there are four points: the way of straying, the sign of having gone astray, the shortcoming of this, and the effect of going astray.

First, the way of straying from the essence. Generally, 'essence' simply means the natural state of your [nondual] awareness — uncontrived and uncor-

44

rupted wakefulness. From primordial beginning until now this wakefulness remains as an empty cognizance that is not made out of anything whatsoever. When, instead of just remaining as that, someone trains in imagining it to be emptiness, he is not free from the conceptual attitude of fixating on emptiness. Therefore he goes astray into what is called 'nihilistic emptiness.'

The sign of having gone astray is to start making statements such as "There are no buddhas above! The are no sentient beings below! Everything is emptiness since it doesn't exist!"

The shortcoming of this way of straying is the conceptual thought, "Everything is emptiness!" Such an attitude makes you abandon all forms of spiritual activity such as devotion and pure perception, refuge and bodhichitta, loving kindness and compassion, and so forth. Instead you become involved in mundane pursuits. With regard to evil, this attitude makes you wantonly engage in unvirtuous actions. Someone who acts in this way of perverting what is true will have no other place to go than Vajra Hell.

Having perverted the truth of what is virtuous, the effect of such demented practice is to take rebirth as someone holding the extreme view of nihilism. Having perverted the truth of cause and effect, you flounder through the ocean of suffering.

Tsogyal, there are many who claim to realize emptiness, but few realize the ultimate natural state.

Now, about 'nature' there are also four points to going astray, of which the first, the way of straying from the nature, is as follows. The natural radiance of empty awareness that is luminously present as kayas and wisdoms has no kayas [bodily forms] with faces and arms, no wisdoms with colors, and is not comprised of any limiting attributes. This natural radiance of emptiness simply remains as a cognizant quality that is indivisible from emptiness. Failing to recognize this cognizant emptiness as an indivisible unity is called 'awareness straying into [dualistic] perception.'

The sign of someone having gone astray in this way is that he phrases all Dharma terms in a extremist manner. Though taught the words describing this unity, his mind cannot grasp them.

The shortcoming of straying in this way is that the conceptual attitude of regarding the perceived [objects] as being concrete prevents you from understanding the teachings of Mind Only. Through strong philosophical partisan-mindedness, you are separated from the paths and stages to omniscience [enlightenment]. He who fixates on what is perceived as being solid reality is not a candidate for liberation!

The effect of this way of going astray, is, outwardly, to take rebirth in the Realms of Form and so forth, due to attributing solidity to manifest luminosity. Inwardly, this one-sided attitude, the failure to recognize awareness as empty cognizance, is not the cause for liberation.

Tsogyal, many claim to have recognized luminosity, but few train in the unity of empty cognizance!

Now, concerning 'capacity' there are four points to going astray, the first of which is the way of straying from the capacity. In essence, no matter how they manifest, the various thoughts that manifest from awareness as the natural radiance of empty cognizance are never beyond being empty awareness. Failure to understand this is called 'straying from empty awareness.'

The sign of having gone astray in this way is that one's thoughts, words and deeds become involved in the [mundane] pursuits of this life.

The shortcoming of this type of straying is that such a conceptual attitude, in which thought occurrence doesn't dawn as dharmakaya, binds you in the web of any arising thought, thus paralyzing your spiritual practice. The predominant negative habits of your latent tendencies make you pursue nothing other than the aims of this life. Caught in the shackles of dualistic doubt, you have chained yourself to hope and fear.

The effect of going astray in this way is to solidify habitual tendencies because of failing to recognize the straying of thoughts; to spend one's life in distraction because of not remembering the consequences of cause and effect; and, when you die, to stray into the three realms.

Many claim to be free of thoughts, but few realize the key point of how they are freed upon arising.

Again Lady Tsogyal asked: Since it is meaningless not to cut through these three ways of straying, how should we transform them?

The master replied: Tsogyal, the empty essence of your awareness is not created by anyone. Without causes and conditions, it is originally present. Don't try to change or alter awareness. Let it remain exactly as it is! Thus you will be free from straying and awaken within the state of primordial purity.

In the same way, your cognizant nature is originally and spontaneously present indivisible from emptiness. Its expression, the unconfined capacity of whatever arises, has no concrete existence. Recognize that all three aspects [of awareness] are a great indivisible unity. Thus you awaken as the indivisibility of the three kayas.

Once more Lady Tsogyal asked: What are the ways of straying from the view, meditation and conduct?

The master replied: Listen here, Tsogyal! First, regarding the view, there are five points: the straying of the view itself, the straying of dwelling place, the straying of companionship, the straying of disturbing emotions, and the straying of one-sidedness.

First, for the straying of the view itself: the general view of the Dharma is to hold that emptiness is beyond limitations, but in this context the yogi of the Heart Essence accepts emptiness to be a direct actuality. When you truly and ultimately achieve realization, these two [emptiness and the experience of actuality] are indivisible. But if you don't, then the general view, which is a view of assumption, doesn't resolve the actual meaning: this is the basic straying of the view. When you have no trust in the view of actuality but instead regard a verbalized view of assumption as being the ultimate, you make statements such as "Everything is beyond reference point, uncreated, and free from extremes!" Behaving in a way that confuses virtue and wrongdoing, you make claims such as "There is no good and evil! There is no benefit from virtuous deeds! There is no harm from wrongdoing! Everything is free and the same!" Thus you remain an ordinary person. This called the 'demonic view of black diffusion,' and it is the root of all ways of straying of the view.

Tsogyal, if you want to avoid going astray in that way, it is essential to act in accordance with the view of nondual, natural cognizance in actuality, inseparable from the conduct of profound cause and effect.

Second, regarding the straying of the dwelling place, it is generally taught that in order to perfect ultimate realization of the view someone who has a temporary realization of it should go to a secluded open area, such as a mountain retreat or a charnel ground. You may temporarily possess the view, but in order to sustain it, you must stay in mountain hermitages. An unwholesome dwelling place may indeed cause your view to go astray.

Tsogyal, if you want to avoid this way of going astray, sustain your temporary view in mountain retreats!

Third, for the straying of companionship, it is generally taught that someone who temporarily has the view should associate with companions who are in harmony with the Dharma and who don't promote disturbing emotions. Keeping company with unwholesome friends, you cannot possibly avoid being influenced by their evil ways. That is the root of going astray since it leads you into pursuing the aims of this life, prevents you from sustaining the view, and increases your disturbing emotions.

Tsogyal, if you want to avoid this way of going astray, cut your ties to superfluous companions and remain in solitude!

Fourth, for the straying of disturbing emotions, someone who temporarily has the view is unable to totally overcome disturbing emotions. He or she becomes involved in disturbing emotions due to a variety of external circumstances. During this involvement, even for one instant, karma is created. If the involvement lasts for a longer duration, you commit negative karmic deeds in the sense that the five poisons create negative karma within each of the six types of perception. Temporarily or ultimately you will reap the effect, so, you must immediately be mindful regardless of which disturbing emotion you feel and relax your attention loosely. Train in loving kindness and compassion for all beings who, out of their disturbing emotions, create karma. Supplicate your master, saying, "Bless me to utilize disturbing emotions as path!" Train daily in the mantra that purifies the seeds of disturbing emotions. Conclude with relaxing into the state of the view and making dedication and aspirations.

If you practice in this way, the good qualities are that you will attain both the temporary and ultimate effects. But if you don't, you sink into the mire of disturbing emotions and fail to perfect the view; that is the most severe root of going astray.

Tsogyal, if you want to avoid going astray in this way, apply the remedy to any disturbing emotion you feel and thus utilize it as your path!

Fifth, regarding the straying of one-sidedness, even people who temporarily possess the view stray into the philosophical position of their own particular school of thought. Drawing quotations from the scriptures, with one-sidedness and prejudice they discriminate between self and other, high and low. Doing so is the basic straying of trying to fathom the great unconfined view of the buddhas with the conceptual attitude of an ordinary person and forming assumptions about it.

Tsogyal, if you want to avoid going astray in such a way, recognize the great unconfined view of freedom!

Regarding the second aspect, the strayings of meditation, there are also five points: the straying of meditation itself, the straying of dwelling place and companionship, the straying of erroneous meditation, and the straying of disturbing emotions.

First, the straying of meditation itself: this is when the disciple fails to understand the direct actuality the master points out. He then goes astray by confusing essence, nature and capacity, and by not recognizing them to be indivisible emptiness and cognizance.

To explain this further: after practicing according to your master's style of oral instructions, if instead you cling to the mere feeling of bliss in body and mind, you will stray into rebirth as a god or human in the Realms of Desire. If you are attached to the state of mind that is merely free of thought, you stray into becoming a god in the Realms of Form. If you are fascinated by being clear and thoughtfree, you stray into becoming a god in the Pure Abodes. If you are attached to being blissful and nonconceptual, you stray into becoming a god in the Realms of Desire. If you are fascinated by being empty and nonconceptual, you stray into becoming a god in the Formless Realms. In these ways you go astray into the three realms.

If you interrupt the flow of sense objects, you stray into the perception-sphere of Infinite Space. If you interrupt sensations, as in the case of deep sleep, you stray into the perception-sphere of Nothing Whatsoever. If you interrupt the perceived while cognizance is still vivid, you stray into the perception-sphere of Infinite Consciousness. If you retain a slight sense of bliss while there continuously is nothing whatsoever perceived, you stray into the perception-sphere of Neither Presence Nor Absence. These are called 'falling into one-sided shamatha,' and when you die and transmigrate, you continue going around within the three realms among the six classes of beings.

Tsogyal, there is no need to fall back into samsara, so, cut through the strayings of foolish meditation practice!

Furthermore, if you believe in the way ordinary people see objects and mind, you stray into materialistic ordinariness. If you regard them one-sidedly as either existent or nonexistent, you stray into the eternalism or nihilism of heretical extremists. If you believe that objects exist separate from mind, you stray into being a shravaka or pratyekabuddha. If you claim that perceptions are mind, you stray into being a Mind Only follower. If you believe that the world and beings are deities, you stray into Mantra. What is the use of meditation practice without knowing how to cut through these strayings!

Well, please give me the method of how to cut through going astray, she asked.

The master replied: Tsogyal, if you want to avoid going astray in these ways, first gain extensive learning; next, concentrate on the pointing-out instruction; and finally, when applying it in practice, understand the above-mentioned ways of straying are nothing other than clinging and attachment to the meditation state. To meditate like the example of a rabbit sleeping in a hawk's nest or with the concentration of an archer is not the cause for liberation. No matter what kind of temporary experience you have, simply relax and remain in whatever is experienced, without trying to improve or alter, without hope and fear, and without accepting and rejecting. When free from fixating on whatever is experienced, there is no cause for going astray.

Second, for teaching the straying of dwelling place and companionship, the meditator should train in a place with the right characteristics. If you stay in a temple of distractions or a place that increases the web of disturbing emotions, your attachment and aversion will cause you to be overcome by these emotions due to moral defilement and the donations you receive. Keeping company with unwholesome friends blocks progress in meditation and is like buying your own poison.

Tsogyal, if you want to practice the Dharma in an authentic way, it is most important to cut your ties to unwholesome places, companions, and so forth. So give them up!

Third, regarding the straying of erroneous meditation, when trying to sustain the meditation state you may experience dullness, agitation, and diffusion[5]. Concerning dullness, there are six kinds: dullness due to location, due to companionship, due to time, due to food, due to posture, and due to meditation.

First, dullness due to location occurs because of staying in a low-lying forest or gorge, or in an area or village of moral defilement. You feel mentally obscured, the bindus are unclear, awareness feels clouded over, you feel very sleepy, and your body feels heavy. In these cases, do cleansing rituals and make confessions; go to open and lofty places; meditate in a place with cloudless, clear sky; open the window for fresh air; imagine that you are at the summit of a snow mountain and have been hit by a fresh breeze. These methods will clear it.

Second, dullness due to companionship occurs when staying with someone of moral defilement or with a consort of impure character who may have been promiscuous. You yourself become defiled. In those cases, exert yourself in the rituals for fulfillment and confession and for purification. Be on guard against people with broken samayas or moral defilement. Seek a qualified consort, let him or her receive empowerment, and don't permit promiscuity. That will clear it.

Third, dullness due to time involves feeling obscured and drowsy in the spring or summer, and is cleared by going to snow mountains and similar places.

Fourth, dullness due to food and clothing involves feeling dull and clouded over from other people's food or defiled garments. When practicing you should keep away from other people's food and defiled garments. That will clear it.

Fifth, dullness due to posture, is when a beginner becomes drowsy from lying down and the like. At the time of meditation practice keep to the three postures or the vajra [cross-legged] position, invigorate your mind, brighten your senses, and meditate with vivid clarity. That will clear it.

Sixth, dullness due to meditation comes from meditating with a depressed frame of mind, thus feeling totally obscured and drowsy. Direct your eyes into the sky, and in a balanced way make yourself keenly awake and sharpen your awareness. That will clear it.

The texts on the gradual stages of the path teach that dullness and agitation are due to the fault of failing to activate awareness. Tsogyal, the hindrances of meditation are not cleared away unless you are diligent!

Next, about agitation, there are two kinds: agitation due to location and agitation due to circumstances. Agitation due to location occurs when, meditating in a clear and lofty place, your awareness becomes brightened, your attention unsettled and your thoughts agitated and scattered. If you let go into whatever catches your attention, you fall prey to disturbing emotions. To deal with this, direct your gaze to the meeting point between earth and sky. If that doesn't calm you down, then apply the [downward] gaze of a shravaka, and sometimes focus your mind on an object. At night, go to sleep while imagining that your mind enters a black bindu, within two egg-shaped channel-junctures located in the soles of your feet. This is one teaching, but it is better to focus your mind on the letter A in your secret place. When a thought suddenly occurs, recognize it, use PHAT, and retain the breath; after that, relax completely and let be. Alternately, pursue the thinker and then rest in the state of not finding one. That will clear it.

Agitation due to circumstances occurs when because of an external incident, you follow a thought, and your mind becomes agitated and scatters into a disturbing emotion. When that happens, keep the attitude of "There is no need to do anything!" Train in loving kindness and compassion, disenchantment, means and knowledge, and devotion. Following that, persevere in the practice as at the time of the view. That will clear it.

The third point, about the fault of diffusion, has two parts: diffusion due to lack of understanding and diffusion due to circumstances. Diffusion due to lack of understanding is when there is no progress no matter how much you meditate. This is because of not knowing how to divide the practice into sessions. You turn against the instruction and your master; or, not knowing how to distinguish between theory and experience, you turn into a stupid meditator.

To deal with this, supplicate your master; develop certainty in the oral instructions; divide your practice into sessions and repeat them numerous times. Without getting involved in activities, meditate openly and freely. When feeling clear, cut thought diffusion and continue meditating. That will cut through diffusion and increase experience.

Second, diffusion due to circumstances occurs when because of some external incident you fall into the five poisons or six types of perceptions, become distracted and lose mindfulness. To deal with this, apply the remedy immediately, cut to pieces the fixation on the perceived, and regard it as a magical illusion.

Tsogyal, if you want to cut through these strayings, club the pig-snout of disturbing emotions!

Fourth, regarding the straying of disturbing emotions: the person who tries to sustain the meditation training will meet numerous enemies and thieves —

his own disturbing emotions. These can be classified into five categories: anger, pride, desire, envy, and delusion. From these roots arise the 84,000 disturbing emotions which won't let you remain in meditation. Each of these five poisons involves you in the five disturbing emotions, which drag you further into samsara. So guard against being distracted by them with the vigilant attitude of a mother who has lost her only child. Abandon these emotions, like discovering a poisonous snake on your lap. Recognize them, alert and mindful, and practice in the same way as when training in the view. Unless you practice in this way, evil karma is created every moment.

Tsogyal, if you want to avoid this way of going astray, exert yourself with skillful warfare against the five poisons, by correctly accepting and rejecting, without being apart from the guard of conscientiousness!

In any case, as long you have not reached some stability in the view and meditation, it is essential to escape into solitude like a wounded deer. Flee from disturbing emotions as if having met a poisonous snake.

Again Lady Tsogyal asked: Shouldn't a practitioner of Secret Mantra take all disturbing emotions as the path?

The master replied: Of course they should be brought onto the path! But only a peacock can feed on poison. The person who is able to take disturbing emotions as path without abandoning them is rarer than the udumvara flower. While for someone of the highest caliber a disturbing emotion manifests as a helper, for a person of lesser capacity it becomes a poison. For this lesser type of person, it is more profound to abandon disturbing emotions!

After how much abandoning does one become adept?, she asked.

When you are not attached to disturbing emotions and sense-pleasures and they are experienced as magical illusions, then you needn't suppress disturbing emotions even when they do arise, as they don't harm. When they don't arise, you have no desire to produce them as you are free from expectations. When that happens, disturbing emotions have been brought onto the path. To try to utilize disturbing emotions as path while not having turned away from clinging to solid reality is like a fly becoming stuck in honey.

Tsogyal, cut through straying in these ways!

The third topic, straying from conduct, has two parts: the straying of untimely conduct, and the general straying of conduct.

The first has seven points. At the beginning, the bee-like conduct should precede learning, reflection and meditation. As it is the conduct of a beginner, it is wrong to follow it at the time for yogic discipline.

The deer-like conduct is exclusively for the time of practicing the path. It is wrong if followed at the time for yogic discipline because your samadhi loses its freedom.

The mute-like conduct is exclusively for the time of having reached the key point of experience. It is wrong if followed when one should behave like a bee, because of not distinguishing between word and meaning.

The conduct of a swallow seeking its nest is exclusively for when you have gained personal experience. It is wrong if followed when you have gained proficiency in samadhi, because it becomes an obstacle.

The madman-like conduct is exclusively for when you have stabilized experience. It is wrong if followed when you only have partial experience, because of not having discovered the full meaning.

The lion-like conduct is exclusively for the time of having perfected the view. It is wrong if followed when trying to gain experience, because, not having found confidence in thatness, you can be overwhelmed by other phenomena.

The conduct that is like dogs and pigs is exclusively for the time of mastery. It is wrong if followed at the wrong time because you will reap the punishment of the dakinis.

When you follow an uncorrupted way of conduct, your personal experience will dawn as the innate nature of dharmata. Having attained mastery over the elements, you can transform the faithless perception of other people, revive the dead, and perform any miraculous feat. If you pervert the above-mentioned ways of conduct, it is called straying from the conduct and you will have no result.

Tsogyal, if you want to avoid going astray in this way, follow the correct way of conduct as described in the scriptures!

Second, regarding the general straying of conduct, you may temporarily fabricate a mode of behavior but that is not in accord with the Dharma. If it doesn't become the path of enlightenment it is called hypocrisy and constitutes a straying of conduct.

Tsogyal, if you want to avoid going astray concerning conduct in general, make sure that whatever behavior you follow becomes the path of enlightenment!

For the fourth topic, the straying of fruition, there are two points: the temporary and the ultimate. First, temporary straying is when, after having practiced the oral instructions, you regard an ordinary result as being the supreme and then feel proud and conceited. This is called a straying because it blocks the ultimate fruition. The ultimate straying is when you fail to dissolve hope and fear even though you have attained the fruition. The effect then strays into being a cause.

Tsogyal, if you want to avoid going astray in this way, recognize that hope and fear have no basis!

Again Lady Tsogyal asked: Does one need to generate bodhichitta after realizing this vital point of seeing in actuality?

The master replied: The greater vehicle and Secret Mantra are indeed distinguished by the special quality of generating bodhichitta. However, unless you remember death, impermanence, cause and effect, and the defects of samsaric existence during the four parts of the day, the events of this life will quickly fly by.

You may claim to be a Mahayana follower, but unless you continuously train in loving kindness and compassion for all sentient beings, you have already strayed into being a shravaka or pratyekabuddha.

You may have high realization, but unless you correctly accept or reject every moment even the minutest aspect of cause and effect, you will still meet with a variety of painful situations.

Tsogyal, if you want to practice the Dharma in an authentic way, connect yourself with realization and what I just mentioned here!

Again Lady Tsogyal asked: What is the greatest obstacle when practicing the path?

The master replied: When first entering the path, any circumstance that leads your mind astray is an obstacle. In particular, women are the biggest demons for a man, and men are the biggest demons for a woman. In general, food and clothing are major demons.

Again Lady Tsogyal asked: But isn't the karma-mudra an enhancement for the path?

Guru Rinpoche replied: The mudra-consort who actually enhances the path is rarer than gold!

Woman of evil karma, you give your devotion to lustful men. You cast your pure perception on your sweetheart. You offer your gathering of merit to your lover. You direct your perseverance into family life. You throw your compassion on your out-of-wedlock child. Your revulsion is aimed at the sacred Dharma. Your daily practice is to cultivate lust. Your essence-mantra is to engage in smutty talk. Your gesture of homage is to make flirtatious signs. Your circum-ambulations are to roam to the place of your fancy. Your fortitude is given to the activity of passion. You try to destroy your delusion with your lower torso. You give your confidence to your secret lover. Your gratitude is for whomever makes love with the most exertion. Your experience is to discuss the topic of love-making. You would probably take your pleasure with a dog, if it would only obey. Your unwavering ultimate goal is to engage in passion. Rather than attaining enlightenment right now, you choose to enjoy one more time.

Your faith is mere platitude, your devotion insincere, but your greed and jealousy are strong. Your trust and generosity are weak, yet your disrespect and doubt are huge. Your compassion and intelligence are weak, but your bragging and self-esteem are great. Your devotion and perseverance are weak, but you are skilled at misguiding and distorting. Your pure perception and courage is small. You don't keep your samaya-commitments, and you can't offer proper service.

Rather than being a helper for going higher, you are the hook that pulls the practitioner down. You aren't the enhancement of bliss, but the harbinger of prejudice and misery. To take a consort while expecting to be liberated through passion becomes a cause for increasing jealousy and disturbing emotions. To hope that a consort will be the support for improving health will only envelop one in the defilement of broken samayas. A woman who doesn't keep the sama-yas correctly is a demon for the practitioner.

Well, how is a qualified consort?, she asked.

The master replied: In general, it is someone without the faults just men-tioned. In particular, it is someone who has interest in the Dharma, is intelligent and good-natured, who has great faith and compassion, possesses the complete six paramitas, doesn't break the master's word, has respect for the practitioner, observes the samayas of Secret Mantra as carefully as her own eyes, who is not promiscuous unless she has gained mastery, and who lives neatly and cleanly. To find such a consort becomes a help for the path, but such a being is rare in Tibet. It should be someone like Princess Mandarava.

Again she asked: What is the biggest shortcoming with being promiscuous before having attained mastery?

Guru Rinpoche replied: Even at the time of mastery it is not appropriate to enjoy without your guru's permission. Aside from the master who confers empowerment, it is also not appropriate for a Dharma brother or a family member to enjoy someone claimed by a practitioner. If he does, the samaya-bond becomes impure in this life, and he is punished by the dakinis with an inauspicious and short life. The Dharma protectors will leave him, he won't attain accomplishment, and he will meet with various obstacles. The woman, after transmigrating from this life, will take rebirth in the hell of Burning Desire. Women should therefore be careful to guard against promiscuity. When a man enjoys a consort claimed by a vajra master possessing the two or three levels [of precepts], or a Dharma sister with the same samayas, it is called 'poisoning the vessels,' and there is no way to avoid taking rebirth in hell. Even to enjoy someone claimed by an ordinary person has extremely severe consequences. During an empowerment there is no fault with enjoying even the [gurus's] consort or a Dharma sister. If you keep the samayas in this way, you quickly attain all the accomplishments of Secret Mantra.

Tsogyal, if you don't observe the samayas after entering the gateway of Mantra, there is no hope of awakening to enlightenment! I have looked through all of Tibet, but I haven't found anyone besides you who can keep the samayas.

Again Lady Tsogyal asked: Since the greatest obstacle when practicing the Dharma is selfish clinging to food, clothes, and body, please tell me how to abandon these three.

Guru Rinpoche replied: Tsogyal, sooner or later this body will perish. The length of one's life is already determined, but we aren't sure whether we will die young or old. Everyone must die, and I haven't seen anyone yet who escaped death by being attached to his or her beautiful body. Give up all the selfish cherishing of your body and keep to mountain retreats!

As for clothes, even a simple sheepskin cloak will suffice, and one can even live on stones and water, but this doesn't seem to be for Tibetan practitioners!

Again Lady Tsogyal asked: Should I write down all you have said?

Guru Rinpoche replied: If you write it down, it will benefit future generations.

She asked: Well, should it be propagated or concealed? How will it bring benefit? Who will make use of it?

Guru Rinpoche replied: The time for propagating this teaching has not yet arrived, so it should be concealed. When I placed the casket containing the scripture of the Heart Essence on the top of the king's daughter's head, princess Pema Sal, I made the aspiration for it to be her allotted teaching. Several lifetimes after she dies, she will meet again with this teaching. You must conceal it as a terma treasure for that purpose.

Vimalamitra will uphold the teachings of the Heart Essence. The time has come for his disciples. This teaching, which is my Heart Essence, will manifest when the Early Translations are corrupted and about to vanish. It will spread and flourish tremendously but for a short while. In general all teachings of the dark age will flourish widely but last only briefly.

At the end of this age, when people's average life-span is fifty years, the princess will take a human rebirth and be accepted by Nyang Ral [Nyima Özer], a speech-incarnation of the king [Trisong Deutsen]. During the latter part of the life of [Guru] Chöwang, the reincarnation of the king, she will be reconnected to the Dharma. In her following life she will meet this terma treasure containing the oral instructions of the Heart Essence. As it will be the time for practice there will not be any activity for the benefit of beings. This person[6] will live for 59 years. He will have various positive and negative karmic connections. Some of his disciples will go to the Blissful Realm, while some will take rebirth in the lower realms. This demonstrates the consequence of defiled samayas and it is possible he will die at the age of fifty. He should be on guard against defiling the samayas, and exert himself in making confessions. By doing so he will be able to live his full number of years.

At this point it is possible that a woman blessed by the five classes of dakinis will appear. If she does and he takes her as his consort, he should pray for longevity; then it will be possible for him to remain for more than fifty years.

He will have a disciple, a destined girl marked with a mole, and if he gives her the complete instructions, she will be able to act for the welfare of beings to some extent. If she doesn't appear within that life, she will become his disciple in the following life and attain enlightenment without remainder at the upper part of Kharag.7

If he doesn't bring these instructions to the lower part of Bumtang, but conceals them at their original terma place or within a rock at a place that cannot be shifted by gods or demons, he will reveal them in his following rebirth.

Following that incarnation, he will for a while roam through the sambhogakaya realms, and after that take birth at Tarpaling in Bumtang. Benefiting beings from the age of fifteen, he will disclose numerous termas and perform various types of miracles. He will remain until the age of seventy. Taking five dakinis who have assumed female form as his consorts, his activity for the benefit of beings will blaze forth. He will have a son named Dawa Drakpa, an emanation of Hayagriva, who will also benefit beings. He will sustain the Buddhadharma for 90 years. Since this is his allotted teaching, conceal it as a terma treasure!

Upon [hearing] this, Lady Tsogyal made innumerable prostrations and circumambulations and exerted herself in writing this down.

Samaya. Seal. Seal. Seal.

Amazing that someone like me, the unintelligent woman Tsogyal,
Should meet with the nirmanakaya through pure aspirations!
Through my pure samaya I have received the quintessence of
    instructions.
By offering my service, he regarded me with loving compassion.
Seeing me a worthy recipient, he entrusted me with the essence of
    Mantra,
And bestowed upon me the supreme, quintessential Heart Essence.
Not expounding it in an untimely fashion, I hid it as a terma treasure.
May this *Golden Rosary of Nectar* in the form of questions and answers
Meet with this person possessing the complete signs!

Samaya.
Seal of profundity. Seal of treasure. Seal of [unreadable]. Seal of severity.

In the dark age this secret cycle of pith instruction,
Is entrusted to a destined one of the water element born in the Year of
the Hare,
A heart son of Uddiyana, possessing a hidden destiny,
A layman with true intelligence,
Whose full powers will not bloom in that life, but will follow a hidden
lifestyle,[8]
Who has unbridled conduct, free from hypocrisy,
Who possesses powerful abilities, but whose power is not revealed,
And who is marked by a mole on the body and has bulging eyes.
His disciples, children of the five classes of dakinis,
Born in the five years of the Tiger, Hare, Dog, Dragon, and Ox,
Will hold his lineage and proceed to the celestial realms.
Whoever holds his lineage will attain buddhahood in one life;
They will be yogis in their last incarnation.

ITHI. May this be virtuous!

SONGS TO THE 25 DISCIPLES:

◈

THE KING AND THE 25 DISCIPLES then asked the precious master of Uddiyana: Please bestow upon us a profound instruction that touches the essential point, which is all-inclusive and yet simple to practice.

Padmasambhava sang in reply:

Amazing!
King, princes and the rest of you disciples,
The true meaning is not within the domain of everyone.
When heard by an unworthy recipient
It becomes the cause of slander, misunderstanding, and damaged
    samayas.

I have given you important prophecies about the future,
But the wicked chieftains of Tibet
Have no trust no matter how much they hear,
Spreading falsehood, they indulge in idle talk.

Nevertheless, I will briefly explain
What you, out of devotion, have asked me.
Now is not the time for propagating,
But for each of you to correctly practice by yourselves.

Since this teaching will be concealed as a terma treasure for the benefit of
    the future,
Take the oath of secrecy!

Instructing them to adhere to this command of secrecy, he first spoke to
the king:

Your Majesty, listen here, take the cross-legged position,
Keep your body straight on the seat and meditate!
Keep your attention thoughtfree and unconfined by mental constructs.
As your focus transcends all types of objects,
Unfixed on any mark of concreteness,
Remain quiet, tranquil and awake!
When you remain like this, the signs of progress naturally appear,
As the clarity of consciousness that neither arises nor ceases
And as awareness utterly free of misconceptions.
This is the awakened state found in yourself,
Not sought elsewhere but self-existing — how wonderful!

Listen here, devoted Tsogyal of Kharchen!
Since your mind has no real identity to be shown,
In a natural, uncontrived, spontaneously present state,
Remain undistracted within the sphere of nonmeditation!
Remaining like this, liberation occurs spontaneously.
This itself is the awakened state!

Listen here, Palgyi Senge, my eminent noble son!
All phenomena of samsara and nirvana are your own mind,
And do not appear apart from this mind —
Devoid of a self-nature, beyond thought, word, and description.
Don't accept the pleasant or reject the awful, don't affirm or deny, make
    no preferences,
But remain vividly awake in the state of unfabricated naturalness!
By remaining like this, the sign of progress is that your body, speech and
    mind
Feel free and easy, beyond the confines of pleasure and pain.
That is the moment of understanding the awakened state!

Listen here, Vairochana, worthy being!
All that appears and exists, samsara and nirvana, arises from your own
      mind —
A mind that cannot be grasped, free from center and edge.
In the natural state of vast equality, intrinsic and uncontrived,
Remain undistracted in great effortlessness!
Whatever thought you think, it arises as the space of wakefulness —
The Awakened One is nothing other than this.
When self-cognizant wakefulness is fully actualized,
That is what is given the name 'buddha!'

Listen here, Yudra Nyingpo from Gyalmo!
Your mind is nonarising, no thing whatsoever is seen.
Thoughtfree, forming no concepts, don't follow your thinking!
So don't affirm or deny, but remain, released in yourself!
In this state, the flow of thought is cut
And wisdom unfolds, drawing the line between samsara and nirvana!

Listen here, Namkhai Nyingpo, mendicant from Nub!
Your mind is simplicity free from ego and a self,
So remain in its self-occurring, self-subsiding state, free from artifice!
At that moment, bliss arises from within,
The signs of progress occur spontaneously; this is itself the awakened
      state!

Listen here, Jnana Kumara, listen undistractedly to this instruction!
Your mind was at first not created through causes,
And at the end will not be destroyed by conditions,
So remain effortless in the indescribable and uncontrived state!
At that moment, the fruition is discovered in yourself without seeking.
Apart from this you will find no other Awakened One!

Listen here, Gyalwa Cho-yang of Nganlam!
The awakened mind of enlightenment is not created through meditation,
So, free from thinking, without projecting or dissolving thought,
Remain with wide-open senses, letting your thinking subside in itself!

Within this state, your thinking spontaneously dissolves
And the wisdoms occur by themselves without being sought.
This is itself the discovering of the awakened state!

Listen here, Dorje Dudjom of Nanam!
That which bears the name 'awakened mind of enlightenment'
Is intrinsic, primordially self-existing and without center or edge.
Don't correct it, but in the state that is self-cognizant and naturally
    serene,
Don't change, don't alter, but remain, released into naturalness!
By remaining like this, your mind free of turmoil
Is itself the Awakened One!

Listen here, Yeshe Yang of Ba, and train in this instruction!
Your mind is unshakable when unfixed on subject and object.
Undistracted by effort, hope and fear, protecting and dissolving
    thoughts;
Don't correct them, but remain in your natural state.
Not to stir from that is itself the Awakened One!

Listen here, Palgyi Yeshe of Sogpo!
The awakened state of mind is unmade,
Unsought and self-existing.
Without the effort of holding a subject and object,
Remain in the unfabricated state of natural cognizance!
By remaining in this way, the stream of agitation is cut and ceases;
Recognize that moment to be the Awakened One!

Listen here, Nanam Yeshe, young mendicant from Shang!
Leave your attention free of dualistic action, don't affirm or deny,
But remain in uncontrived effortlessness, don't accept or reject.
The awakened state is to dwell undistractedly in that!

Listen here, Palgyi Wangchuk of Kharchen!
Leave your mind in nonmeditation, don't fabricate an attitude,
But, without constructing, remain in self-existing natural cognizance!

By remaining in that state, without casting samsara aside,
The natural dissolving of samsara's faults is the wisdom of the Awakened
    One!

Listen here, Denma Tsemang, eminent being!
Your mind is devoid of subject and object and is not made,
So, free from effort and artifice, don't create anything through
    meditation,
But remain undistracted in self-existing natural cognizance!
By remaining in that state, natural cognizance is liberated.
You will never find the Awakened One if you abandon this!

Listen here, translator Kawa Paltsek of Chinbu!
When letting go of subject and object, the mind is not a thing to show.
Likewise, it is not to be made or corrected.
Remain in the state of equanimity, not straying into fixation on
    concreteness.
Remaining undistracted from that is itself the awakened state!

Listen here, Palgyi Senge of Shubu!
The awakened state of mind is free from all claims to be more or less.
Unfabricated and naturally free from the subject that accepts or rejects an
    object,
Don't dwell on anything, be utterly unobstructed.
To remain in this state is itself the Awakened One!

Listen here, Gyalwey Lodrö, mendicant of Drey!
Your mind cannot be thought of, nor can it be observed.
It lies beyond being and not being, permanence and annihilation,
So remain free of the meditation on meditator and object!
When you remain undistracted from that state,
That is what is called the dharmakaya of the Awakened One!

Listen here, Lokyi Chungpa, to this instruction!
Leave your attention free of knower and known,
Do not fixate, but relax freely without wishing,

And remain in the state of cognizance devoid of self-nature.
To remain unwavering from that is itself the awakened state!

Listen to this, Drenpa Namkha!
Your mind, which perceives yet is free of substance,
Cognizes without thought, is conscious yet indescribable.
Free from the movements of conceptual thinking,
Remain in that state, awake and wide-open.
To remain in this nature is itself the awakened state!

Listen here, Palgyi Wangchuk of O-dren!
Awakened mind is a perceiving emptiness, an empty yet luminous
    cognizance.
Remain in its self-existing state, don't alter or correct it.
To remain unmoved from that is itself the Awakened One!

Listen to this, Rinchen Chok!
The identity of your attention, which consists of nothing whatsoever,
Is not to be held; neither is it to be created or neglected in meditation.
Don't correct or alter its self-existing freshness,
But remain in the original state that is spontaneously present!
Within this state, don't let your mind waver,
Since you will never find a fruition apart from this!

Listen here, Sangye Yeshe, mendicant from Nub!
Awakened mind is empty while perceiving
And likewise perceives while being empty.
An inconceivable unity of perceiving and aware emptiness —
Remain in naturalness, undistracted from this sphere.
To remain unmoved from this is itself the Awakened One!

Listen here, Palgyi Dorje Wangchuk of Lhalung!
The nature of your mind is not concrete and has no attributes,
Don't seek to fabricate or improve it, but remain without changing or
    forgetting.
To remain like that is itself the Awakened One!

Listen here, Könchok Jungney of Langdro!
Your mind is inconcrete and primordially pure,
Naturally empty and uncontrived,
So remain in the state free from meditator and meditation object.
Through this, you attain the fruition of buddhahood!

Listen here, Gyalwa Jangchub of Lasum!
Your mind does not arise or cease, nor does it have attributes of
    concreteness.
Empty by nature, its cognizance is unobstructed.
To remain unmoved from this is itself the Awakened One!

All of you, apply these instructions in your experience!
You may compare the sutras and tantras of the Buddha and their
    commentaries,
With words in numbers that transcend the limits of space,
But the concise meaning is included in just these vital points.
So practice them, and hide them as treasures in accordance with your
    oath!

    Thus Padmasambhava spoke, and by merely bestowing the true essential instruction upon them, they were all liberated and attained accomplishment.

THE TREASURY OF
PRECIOUS JEWELS
TO DISPEL
HINDRANCES:

REPLIES TO QUESTIONS FROM YESHE TSOGYAL

IN THE HERMITAGE OF SAMYE CHIMPHU, Lady Tsogyal, the Princess of Kharchen, implored the master Padmakara: Please pay heed, great master! Although you have shown an unintelligent girl like me that all of the world and its beings are dharmakaya, still my Dharma practice strays into theoretical understanding due to my continuous company with the habit of deluded perception. I beg you: kindly bestow upon me the instruction to enable me to join whatever I do with the innate nature of dharmata!

Padmasambhava replied: Tsogyal, listen! You must possess these three key points when practicing the Secret Mantra teachings of the greater vehicle: the key point of the body, the posture; the key point of the eyes, the gaze; and the key point of the mind, the way of resting.

First of all, in a secluded place, sit in the cross-legged position upon a comfortable seat, rest your arms in equanimity, and straighten your backbone. If your body remains in its original state, meditation occurs naturally. Without assuming the physical posture, meditation doesn't happen.

Next, for the gaze, don't close your eyes, blink or glare sideways. Look directly and unwaveringly ahead. Since the eyesight and the consciousness share a single nature, meditation occurs naturally. Without the right gaze meditation doesn't happen.

The key point of mind is this: don't let the natural state of your ordinary mind pursue past habitual patterns, don't let it look forward to future activities of disturbing emotions, and don't let it fabricate anything in your present state by conceptualizing. Through resting consciousness in its natural mode, meditation occurs naturally. If you are distracted or diffused, meditation doesn't happen.

When in this way you let your three doors rest in their natural state, all gross and subtle thoughts subside and your mind remains loosely in itself. That is called shamatha, resting calmly. [When your mind is] unobstructed, locationless, and naked in spontaneous wakefulness [that is called vipashyana].[9] When these two, in a conscious instant, stay vividly clear as an indivisible identity, that is called shamatha inseparable from vipashyana. Intellectual understanding is when you keep consciousness as an object. Experience is when you discover its locationlessness, and realization occurs when these states of mind remain vividly clear as the essence of your meditation practice. This is not any different than the realization of the buddhas of the three times. It is not a fabrication based on the master's profound instructions, nor a result of a disciple's sharp intelligence. It is called arriving at the natural state of the ground.

When meditating in this way, the three experiences of bliss, clarity and nonthought arise.

Consciousness free from conceptual thinking is called nonthought and has three types. 'No good thought' means free from clinging to meditator and meditation object. 'No evil thought' is the interruption of the flow of gross and subtle conceptual thinking. 'No neutral thought' is the recognition of the natural face of awareness as being locationless.

During this state of nonthought, clarity is the unobstructed, naked radiance of awareness. There are three types of clarity. 'Spontaneous clarity' is the state of being free from an object. 'Original clarity' does not appear for a temporary duration. 'Natural clarity' is not made by anyone.

There are four types of bliss. 'Blissful feeling' is to be free from adverse conditions of disharmony. 'Conceptless bliss' is to be free from the pain of concepts. 'Nondual bliss' is to be free from the clinging of dualistic fixation. 'Unconditioned bliss' is to be free from causes and conditions.

When these types of experience arise, you need the three analogies of detachment: detachment from bliss is like a madman; detachment from clarity is like the dream of a small child; and detachment from nonthought is like a yogi who has perfected his yogic discipline. When you possess these, you are free from the defects of meditation.

If you are fascinated by and cling to these three experiences, you stray into the three states of existence. When clinging to bliss you stray into the realm of desire; when clinging to clarity you stray into the realm of form; and when clinging to nonthought you stray into the formless realm.

Even though you think you are neither attached nor clinging to them you retain a subtle internal attachment. To cut through this pitfall there are the 'nine serene states of successive abiding,' beginning with the four dhyana states of serenity for discarding the thought of desire. The first dhyana is to be free from the conceptual thinking of perceiver and perceived, but to still be involved in discerning an object and act of meditation. The second dhyana is to be free from conceptual thinking and discernment, while still fixating on savoring the taste of the samadhi of joy. The third dhyana is to attain unmoving mind, but with inhalation and exhalation. The samadhi of the fourth dhyana involves being totally free from conceptual thinking with unobstructed clear perception.

The four formless states of serenity eliminate the conceptual thinking of the realm of form. Dwelling on the thought, "all phenomena are like space!" you stray into the [perception-sphere of] Infinite Space. Dwelling on the thought, "consciousness is infinite and directionless!" you stray into Infinite Consciousness. Dwelling on the thought, "the clear cognizance of perception is not present, not absent, and cannot be made an object of the intellect!" you stray into Neither Presence Nor Absence. Dwelling on the thought, "this mind does not consist of any entity whatsoever; it is nonexistent and empty!" you stray into the perception-sphere of Nothing Whatsoever. These states possess the slight defilement of being conceptualizations, mental fascinations, and experiences of dualistic mind.

The serenity of cessation discards the concepts of all these states. Analytical cessation is the ceasing of the six consciousnesses' engagement with their objects, which involves evenly resting in the interruption of the movement of breath and dualistic mind. Non-analytical cessation is to arrive at your innate nature. That is ultimate indifference.

Among the nine states of serenity, the four dhyana states are 'the shamatha that produces vipashyana.' Thus, the samadhi of these four *dhyanas* is in harmony with the innate nature and the most eminent among all types of mundane samadhi.

The four formless states of serenity are pitfalls of samadhi. The serenity of cessation is the peaceful samadhi of a shravaka.

By recognizing these states you can distinguish the different types of samadhi, clear away the hindrances in your meditation practice and avoid going astray.

The five paths are included within three. Having cut through these pitfalls and practiced a flawless meditation, you remain serenely and vividly in bliss, clarity and nonthought during the meditation state.[10] In the post-meditation state, appearances arise unobstructedly and are as insubstantial as a dream or magical illusion. You understand the nature of cause and effect, fill the measure of merit to the brim, attain the 'heat of samadhi', and thus perfect the path of accumulation.

By practicing like that for a long time, you see in actuality, locationless and self-cognizant, the nature present in yourself. Recognizing your natural face is the path of seeing. Experiencing appearance, awareness and emptiness to be locationless and self-cognizant, you see directly the unconditioned innate nature. The obscuration of disturbing emotions is destroyed at its root. Realizing that cause and effect are empty, samsara has no solid existence. This is called the first bhumi of the Joyous. The meditation state is indivisible from buddhahood, and everything in the post-meditation state arises as magical illusion.

Growing familiar with this state and sustaining it steadily, all phenomena become nondual. Recognizing them as self-display, appearances and mind mingle into one. When emptiness arises as cause and effect, you realize dependent origination. During the meditation state all phenomena are locationless and present as the essence of awareness. The slight presence of objective appearances during the post-meditation state is the path of cultivation.

Maintaining this for a long time, you realize that all of samsara and nirvana is nondual, beyond arising and ceasing, unmixed and utterly perfect, locationless and self-cognizant. The cognitive obscuration totally vanishes, and the very moment everything dawns as original wakefulness is the path of consummation, the state of buddhahood.

Again Tsogyal asked: Please pay heed, great master! This is the innate nature of things, but how should one behave until attaining stability?

Padmasambhava replied: Listen, Tsogyal! There are three types of conduct. First of all, to establish the path there is the common conduct that is general. Next, to bring forth enhancement, there is the secret conduct of yogic discipline. Finally, there is the ultimate conduct of true thatness.

Conduct is very important because much of life is spent in the daily activities of post-meditation. You may have intellectually understood a high view, but unless you act in accordance with its meaning you stray from the path. You may have gained an excellent state of meditation, but unless you sustain it during the activities of post-meditation it will fade away. Understand therefore the vital point of cause and effect: avoid evil deeds, and perform even the most minute virtuous actions. That is the correct path, the essence of the Buddha's teachings, the crucial point of knowledge.

If, having obtained a human body, you want to practice the sacred Dharma correctly, do not let your three doors stray into ordinariness even for an instant. During daytime practice leave your consciousness unfabricated and let the six senses experience freely, like a dream or a magical illusion. At night, mingle deep sleep with dharmata in a nonconceptual state free from projecting or dissolving thoughts. Purify the deluded experience of the dream state, turning it into the correct path. That is to say, train in love, compassion and bodhichitta, and in growing familiar with the stages of development and completion.

Morning and evening, perform the sevenfold purity[11] and do not neglect the daily *torma* offerings and so forth. Confess your misdeeds with the hundred syllable mantra. Be careful about the vital point of cause and effect. Again and again, reflect upon the difficulty of obtaining the freedoms and riches, upon death and impermanence, and upon the defects of samsara.

Train in bodhichitta. Train in the development stage, so that all that appears and exists is the mandala of the deity. For the completion stage, rest in the state of nonduality that is appearance devoid of a self-nature, like the reflection of the moon in water. At the end, dedicate the root of virtue.

Practicing in this way, you are in harmony with the general vehicles, you proceed on the correct path, and you have established the foundation for the path of yoga.

Practice the secret conduct of yogic discipline after you have established the foundation of the path and have gained experience, understanding, and confidence in the view and the true state. The secret conduct enhances that path and cuts through conceptual thinking. It can be pursued by the practitioner who has strong familiarity and stability in practice.

In terms of the correct practice of Mahayana, there is the view of understanding that all objects are unreal. For Secret Mantra, there is the view of the deity circle — the development stage — and nonduality beyond extremes — the completion stage.

When you perceive all sentient beings as your parents, you have given rise to the path through training your mind in bodhichitta. In order to cut through ego-clinging and the belief in demons, go to a frightening place and camp in the most dreadful spot. Begin with taking refuge in the Three Jewels, developing bodhichitta, and supplicating your guru. Then for a long time earnestly cultivate immeasurable love, compassion and bodhichitta for all sentient beings equal to space, headed by the spirit of that locality. Rest and go to sleep in the ultimate bodhichitta, the state of unconstructed great bliss beyond arising, dwelling and ceasing, in which gods and demons are nondual. When you feel fear or dread, concentrate and focus your mind on this reflection: "This fear and dread arises from a belief in demons, which stems from not understanding that all sentient beings are my parents. Now this thought projection appears as demons. How will my bodhichitta, which is merely platitudes and intellectual ideas, accomplish the true meaning?" Focusing your mind like that, cultivate sincere compassion and bodhichitta and surrender your body without concern to all gods and demons, headed by the spirit of that locality. Saying, "Take my flesh, blood and bones, as you please!", rest your mind quietly in bodhichitta.

In the same way, when you have a thought of a god or demon and your bodhichitta wavers, think, "This is a projection made by the belief in demons!" and offer them your body without any concern. Then rest in equanimity. If a ghost should actually appear, jump directly into his mouth or onto his lap and completely surrender the notion of cherishing your body. Cultivate compassion and dedicate the virtue.

When your belief in demons is cut through, demonic manifestations and magical displays subside and the spirit of the locality falls under your control. The subsiding of thought and the taming of demons occur simultaneously.

Once you understand that all sentient beings are your parents, it is impossible to believe in demons, but if you still do, you are not yet fully trained.

Secondly, to cut through,[12] recognize that all objects are unreal. Having cut the belief in demons and the fixation on evil influences as being real, go to the most terrifying place in order to enhance your view of unreal appearances. Take refuge, develop bodhichitta, and supplicate. While recognizing that all objects are unreal, all concepts are delusion, all things are empty, and that your present perception is like a dream or a magical illusion, go to sleep in the state of unconstructed emptiness in which nothing ultimately exists.

When you feel fear, dread or terror, focus your mind, reflecting like this: "Not understanding fear and dread to be like a dream and a magical illusion, I believe in demons. Now this projection has arisen to show me that my view of illusion is only intellectual comprehension. That will not accomplish the true meaning!" Concentrate and focus your mind on this thought and rest freely in the state in which everything is unreal and a magical illusion.

You must recognize the unreal nature of the projection of the belief in demons the very moment the thought or magical display occurs. Decide that it has no reality but is definitely like a magical illusion. If in actuality a ghost appears, resolve that it is unreal and jump directly into its lap. The swirling wind of the demonic appearance will vanish and you move unimpededly through it. The very moment you cut through your belief in demons, the magical display naturally subsides. Overcoming your thought and ending the demons occurs simultaneously.

Third, to cut through, train in a steady development stage whereby your experience manifests as the form of the deity. To enhance your development stage and cut through the belief in demons and the dualistic clinging to a world with beings, go to a frightening place. Once there take refuge, develop bodhichitta, and make supplications. Visualize the environment as a celestial palace, and all sentient beings, especially the spirit of the locality, as the yidam deity.

Recite the essence mantra, sharpen your awareness, brighten your mind and meditate for a long time. Embrace ultimate emptiness with the vital point. Go to sleep within the state in which everything appears and yet is devoid of self-nature. When a thought of fear or dread occurs, focus your mind one-pointedly and reflect in this way: "Failing to recognize a dreadful and terrifying demonic appearance as the yidam, I formed the belief in demons and evil ghosts. Now its projection appears as a magical display. My development stage is only words and intellectual understanding. How will that make me reach accomplishment?" One-pointedly focusing your mind, cast away the fixation of cherishing your body and give it as a feast offering. Visualize vividly that all that appears and exists is the yidam deity.

Consecrate your normal body as nectar and give it to all sentient beings, headed by evildoers. Rest freely in the state of unconstructed nonduality.

The belief in demons arose because as soon as the demonic appearance or magical display occurred, you failed to realize the appearance to be the mandala of the deity. Think, "It is just a projection!", and remember the deity.

Gaining some accomplishment will result in the understanding that you and the demon are of the same identity as the deity. So think, "How delightful it is to meet the yidam!" Embrace the demon [by leaping onto] its lap, enter through its mouth and mingle your minds indivisibly. Present your material body as a feast offering. Through this you will understand that appearances are the deity, and thus all concepts of a demon cease, magical displays naturally subside, and the spirit of the locality falls under your control.

Fourth, to cut through, understand the nature of nonduality by means of a steady view of the completion stage.

Use your fear, dread and belief in demons to enhance the nondual nature of the completion stage. To do so, perform the preliminaries and rest freely in the state of nonduality in which body and mind are nondual, appearance and mind are nondual, self and others are nondual, friend and enemy are nondual, god and demon are nondual. In short, rest in the state where there is no dualistic phenomena whatsoever. Undistractedly sustain that continuity.

If magical displays or the thought of demons occur while practicing like this, focus on nonduality, thinking, "This projection, born from doubt, is due to my mind not remaining one-pointedly in nonduality!" As soon as the belief in demons arises, rest freely in nonduality. If a demon actually appears, focus your mind one-pointedly and think: "How delightful to have the chance to train in the nature of nonduality as an enhancement of the view!" Jump onto the demon's lap, and you will unimpededly move through it in nondual, root-less emptiness. Ultimately the demon does not possess any reality.

In this way the meaning of nonduality dawns in your being. The dualistic thought of believing in demons is interrupted and external magical displays naturally subside. When you realize nonduality you also gain control over evil forces and obstructing demons. This is due to nonduality and the interdepend-ence of appearance and mind.

Consequently, when you are still the demons are also still; when you are pacified, the demons are pacified; when you are liberated, the demons are liber-ated; and when you are tamed the demons are also tamed. The demon is your own demon and cutting through it pacifies yourself. Therefore, it is a greater enhancement to confront a single frightening place than to do three years of meditation.

This secret conduct is not only aimed at the thought of demons but also at cutting through contagious diseases such as leprosy and feelings of fear, dread, repulsion, disgust, timidity, cowardice, embarrassment and so forth. In short, no matter what thought arises, cut through it as above.

Finally, the ultimate conduct of true thatness is free from the duality of gods and demons. Free from the duality of purity and dirt, the knot of dualistic fixation is untied. Free from accepting good or rejecting evil, doubt and hesita-tion are cut through. Free from the impulse to avoid, cultivate or cling, all con-cepts of samsara and nirvana totally vanish into the expanse of nondual wakefulness, and you remain nakedly as nondual unity, the essence of great bliss.

At that time, even if the Dharmaraja, the Lord of Death, puts his hook into you and takes you away, you will not feel fear or dread. Even if Buddha Vajra-sattva himself appears you will not have any doubt or uncertainty to resolve. That itself is called the ultimate conduct of true meaning.

Through these types of secret conduct you establish the foundation of the natural state, enhance the view, refine the practice, and consummate the frui-tion. This teaching is extremely profound.

Again Tsogyal asked: Please pay heed, great master! I implore you, kindly give me a pith instruction that cuts the root of suffering within present wakefulness and brings both birth and death onto the path.

Padmasambhava replied: Listen, Tsogyal! Showing the key points of practice through the five yogas, I shall teach you the pith instruction in using as path whatever you do.

First, for the sleep yoga, the moment of falling asleep resembles dying. Therefore, repair your samayas, retake the shravaka vows, purify your mindstream, cut through the complexity of the three poisonous emotions, and avoid involvement in recollecting and planning. Leave all outer and inner phenomena totally free in the samadhi of suchness, the state of not focusing upon anything whatsoever. To fall asleep in the state of the unconstructed completion stage, the nonconceptual dharmakaya, is to utilize dying as path.

Dissolve all outer and inner phenomena, the world and beings, the chief figure and retinue, into the seed syllable in your heart center. By going to sleep within the state of nonfocus, you utilize the concept of dying as path.

Second, the yoga of awakening resembles taking rebirth. As soon as you wake up, vividly recollect unobstructed awareness from within the completion stage. That purifies taking rebirth.

Next, you should understand the crucial points of cause and effect. This brings vital substance to whatever spiritual practice you do and is a greater enhancement than anything else.

At dawn, distribute the pure part of food into the nadis and excrete the impure portion. When the interior of the nadis is utterly empty, it is easy for outer, inner and secret faults or virtues to arise. The nadis then arise as the central channel, the prana as wisdom [prana], the elements as great bliss, and your mind as nondual wakefulness. This is also the purpose of performing any type of medicinal cure or healing ritual. Moreover, it is the reason why the truly perfected Buddha awakened to true and complete enlightenment at dawn.

Third, the food yoga must be combined with an empowerment of Secret Mantra. If you practice the development stage, consecrate the food as being wisdom nectar. Visualizing the deity within your belly, enjoy the food as a deity dissolving into a deity.

If you practice purifying obscurations, consecrate the food as wisdom nectar. Eat in the manner of completely burning away the seeds of the six classes of beings that are present in the form of letters within your heart.

If you practice union, consecrate the food as being the nectar of nondual means and knowledge, and eat in the manner of uniting.

If you practice the completion stage, consecrate the food as being the wisdom of coemergent appearance and emptiness. Enjoy dharmata eating dharmata.

In short, rest indivisibly in whatever samadhi you are practicing and enjoy. In this way, whatever food you eat becomes a cause for samadhi.

Fourth, regarding the continuous yoga, a practitioner who applies the path correctly should never indulge in ordinary disturbing emotions. He or she should identify all emotions that arise by means of special techniques, and bring them onto the correct path.

The root of disturbing emotions is the five poisons; here is how to use them as path. When strong desire abruptly arises, recognize it by being mindful and, reflect upon its cause. It arose due to an external factor, being swayed by the impulse to have intercourse with an attractive man or woman. At present, the ache of desire is like a violent gush of water. Eventually your mind will entirely dissipate into the pattern of whatever you have grown used to.

To recognize that pattern, understand that the external captivating factor is created by your mind. If that were not so, it would be impossible for your loving friend to be regarded as an enemy by other people. Your impulse to have intercourse arises from your mind and manifests as desire, just like the wind arising out of an empty sky.

Now, here is how to look into the essence of desire and use it as path. Rest in the state in which the attractive external factor and the impulse to have intercourse are free from duality: desire thereby becomes the essence of nondual bliss and emptiness. The innate nature of emptiness is not made out of anything [separate from] its expression, which arises as bliss. This is the perfection of desire, the individually discriminating wisdom.

Likewise, by looking into the essence of anger and resting in that, you realize the nondual essence of clarity and emptiness. The innate nature is empty and its expression is clarity. That is the perfection of anger, the mirror-like wisdom.

By looking into the essence of stupidity and resting in that state, you realize a nonconceptual wakefulness. The innate nature is empty and its expression is nonthought. This perfection of stupidity is the dharmadhatu wisdom.

In the same way, by bringing pride and jealousy onto the path they become the wisdom of equality and the all-accomplishing wisdom.

In short, the ten nonvirtues result from the five poisons. The five poisons come from the three poisons. By recognizing these three poisons and utilizing them as path, you uphold the teachings of the Tripitaka and remain in the three trainings:

By looking into the essence of desire and resting in that state, you experience bliss, which becomes the Vinaya Pitaka. You turn away from ordinary desire, which is the training of discipline.

By looking into the essence of anger and resting in that state, you experience clarity, which becomes the Sutra Pitaka. You turn away from ordinary anger, which is the training of samadhi.

By looking into the essence of stupidity and resting in that state, you experience nonthought, which becomes the Abhidharma Pitaka. You turn away from ordinary stupidity, which is the training of discriminating knowledge.

You should recognize all disturbing emotions that arise and in this way bring them onto the path.

Fifth is the yoga of time and vital points. There are five times. First, at dawn the pure and impure part of the food are separated, your mind is sharp, your body refreshed, your intellect clear, and the bindus increased. The force of either faults or virtues is stronger so it is essential to recognize any thought arising as desire and bring it onto the path of virtue.

Secondly, at dusk the power of your bindus wanes, and a feeling of anxiety may arise. The magical displays of gods and demons are greater. This time resembles death. The force of either faults or virtues is stronger, so it is essential to recognize any thought arising as fear and dread and put it to use on the path of virtue.

Third, when a strong disturbing emotion or a turbulent thought arises, if you fail to utilize it as path, it may cost you your life, or cause you to break your vows, obstruct your samadhi, and distort the true path. So, recognize it and bring it onto the path.

Fourth, at the time when nondual original wakefulness arises and your mind is unified as the essence of nonthought, use this on the path of means. While in the state of applying the key points within the framework of those exercises, practice for a long time without a moment of distraction. At that time aspirations and the links of causation are formed. This is a vital point, so it is important to form resolve. Mixing the aspirations and links of causation with any other type of ordinary conceptual thinking is improper. Since the one who forms [an aspiration] is a conceptual thought, it is like the mistake of using a cooling medicine against a cold disease.

Fifth, when the time of death comes you will be completely under the power of your own particular 'linking karma'; therefore, it is crucial to form positive causal links. Let all misdeeds be forgotten, and remember all virtuous actions. Focus your mind one-pointedly upon the particular practice you are stable at, and, every single moment, be free from deluded experience. In short, at this time it is crucial to form a virtuous link of causation.

Tsogyal again asked: Please pay heed, great master! Please teach the key points of the bardo states.

Padmasambhava replied: Listen, Tsogyal! As for the bardo, the period from death until you take rebirth is called the bardo of birth and death. It is comprised of three points: the best is to attain enlightenment before experiencing any bardo; next best is to attain enlightenment in the bardo state; third is how to take rebirth.

The first point has four parts: how the elements dissolve, how the thoughts cease, how nonconceptual wisdom appears, and how buddhahood is attained by recognizing one's nature.

First, when the element of earth dissolves into water, the nadi-knot at the navel disintegrates, the earth-prana malfunctions, the body feels heavy, consciousness fades, and an experience that is like a mirage appears.

Next, when water dissolves into fire, the nadi-knot at the heart disintegrates, the water-prana malfunctions, the mouth and nose dry out, consciousness is restless, and an experience resembling smoke arises.

Third, when fire dissolves into wind the nadi-knot at the throat disintegrates, the fire-prana malfunctions, the body temperature grows faint, perception vacillates, and an experience that is like fireflies arises.

Fourth, when wind dissolves into consciousness the nadi-knot at the secret place disintegrates, the wind-prana malfunctions, the breath stops moving through the nostrils, the consciousness is slightly confused, and a slight appearance of light appears.

How the thoughts cease: at the lower end of the central channel is the essence from our mother in the form of the letter A. When the power of the right channel wanes this essence moves upward: the sign for that is the appearance of redness. At that time the thought states of desire cease.

At the upper end of the central channel is the essence from our father in the form of the letter HANG. When the power of the left channel wanes this essence moves downward and a whiteness appears. At that time the thought states of anger cease.

Following that, the pervading wind at the crown of the head malfunctions and thereby the blackness appears. At that time the thought states of stupidity cease.

When the three poisons have ceased in this way pride and envy will automatically cease, because the three poisons have dissolved into the three nadis. After this, the outer breath stops.

How nonconceptual wisdom appears: up to this point, the outer breath is interrupted but the inner breath has not ceased. The ascending sun and the descending moon meet together and the prana-mind enters the central channel. Because these three remain within the central channel and because thoughts have ceased for a short while, nonconceptual wakefulness, the dharmakaya mind of the buddhas, appears for the length of the period it takes to eat a meal.

How buddhahood is attained by recognizing nonconceptual wisdom: by the power of having grown accustomed to that recognition, and by the power of having gained stability in the oral instructions, you will recognize this self-existing coemergent wisdom and attain buddhahood, uniting the mother and child aspects of dharmakaya. Following this, awareness emerges through the aperture of Brahma and enters dharmadhatu.

That was the instruction for the person of the highest capacity to attain buddhahood without a bardo.

The instruction for the person of intermediate capacity to attain enlightenment in the bardo state has four points. The way in which the elements dissolve and the thought states cease are the same as above.

Regarding the third point, how dharmata manifests in the bardo: if one does not recognize the nonconceptual state of dharmakaya, as in the case of the person of the highest capacity, the awareness abiding in the heart center enters the pathway of the white silk nadi. Emerging outside, mind and matter separate, and you fall unconscious for seven days.[13] Awakening from the faint, dharmata manifests for five days in the form of sounds, colors, lights and spheres.

The sound is the natural sound of the fire element, immense and forceful. It roars like the thunder that divides summer and winter. The natural radiance of awareness manifests in clear and vivid colors. The rays of light shining from within the colors are dazzling like a mirage on the plains at autumn.

Fourth, how buddhahood is attained by recognizing your natural face: by the power of practicing what has been pointed out, these manifestations of sounds, colors, and lights will appear as self-existing coemergent wisdom and you will attain buddhahood.

Individuals differ in their respective training and familiarities. For the yogi who has trained in the completion stage of deity yoga, these manifestations of sounds, colors, and lights will unfold as the natural manifestation of the deity's mandala, and he will attain buddhahood as a sambhogakaya.

The yogi who has realized the falsity of appearances will understand that these manifestations of sounds, colors, and lights are like a dream or a magical illusion and will attain buddhahood as a nirmanakaya.

The yogi who has recognized that all the phenomena of samsara and nirvana are individual experience (*rangnang*) will understand that these manifestations of sounds, colors, and lights are self-arising and self-liberated, and will attain buddhahood as the essence kaya.

Therefore, you should cross the bardo by means of whichever practice you have gained experience and realization in.

Lastly, the matter of how to take rebirth has five points. The way in which the elements dissolve and the thought states cease are similar to the foregoing.

Third, the mental body is formed gradually through this eightfold dependent origination:[14] Ignorance is failing to recognize that the light is your own self-display (*rangnang*). Formation occurs, by the power of this, when the five pranas gather and form samsaric existence. From this, consciousness grows clearer and fixation on an object takes place. Next, the name-and-form of the bardo state arises.15 Consciousness becomes sharper and faster, forming the sense bases. Contact is when they meet with an object. Sensation is the feeling of pleasure or pain. Craving is when you thereby give rise to like or dislike. Thus, these eight factors form the mental body.

Fourth, how the bardo experience takes place: the appearances of former habitual tendencies and karma manifest; thus you experience traveling to your former country and home and mentally keep company with all your close relatives. Your food and dwelling place are uncertain, and your mental body lives off burnt offerings. Apart from being able to enter the womb of the mother of your next rebirth and approach the Vajra Seat, you can move unobstructedly. Constantly afraid, scared and in panic, you experience the visions of flesh-eating demons, ferocious wild animals, torrential rainstorms and blizzards. You seek refuge and a hiding place everywhere. Your sense bases are clear and the mental faculty is intact. You possess pure divine sight and can see other bardo beings.

Fifth, how to take the next rebirth: After the previous self-radiance of basic luminosity has subsided, you experience the five ordinary light-paths.16 Co-emergent ignorance is failing to recognize [this luminous wakefulness as being] your natural face. Conceptual ignorance is conceptualizing the luminosity as being something other. Fixating upon this appearance of other, you take rebirth among the six classes of beings, like a mountain deer caught in a snare or a honeybee stuck in a flower.

Fixating upon the white light, you will be reborn among the hell beings; fixating upon the red, you will take birth as a hungry ghost. Entering the black light leads to birth as an animal, while to enter the yellow leads to birth as a human being, and to fixate upon the green leads to rebirth as a god or demigod. At that time you must remember the sufferings of the six classes of beings and not fixate on any of these lights.

The bardo consciousness easily changes direction, so if you can remain mindful and generate deep yearning towards a buddhafield such as Sukhavati you will take rebirth there without a doubt.

Tsogyal again asked: Please pay heed, great master! Shouldn't the yogi who hasn't attained stability exert himself in clearing hindrances? How does one clear away the hindrances of the path?

Padmasambhava replied: Listen, Tsogyal! Clearing the hindrances from the path has four points: clearing the hindrance of samadhi's temporary experiences, clearing the hindrance of bodily sickness and pain, clearing the hindrance of conceptual thinking and gods and demons in the mind, and clearing the hindrance of temporary defilement due to negative circumstances.

First, clearing the hindrance of samadhi's temporary experiences: dullness means failing to actualize radiant awareness, failing to embrace it with the experience of clarity. Dullness is mixed with sleep, due to drowsiness.

Agitation means the consciousness moves out towards an object or in pursuit of something. 'Moving out' means the attention doesn't remain quiet. To be diffused is to get caught up in the perception of something other. Being unsettled is being quiet for a short time but unable to remain so for long. 'Undercurrent' is your attention moving unnoticed while you think that it remains still.

Agitation is of two types. 'Agitation by something other' means that the consciousness becomes agitated due to some circumstance. 'Agitation by oneself' means that a subtle feeling of thinking "It's quiet! It's clear!" enters the meditation state.

Dullness and agitation are the primary faults that arise from failing to concentrate and slipping into indifference.

When feeling dull, direct your attention to the heart center. Remain focused and concentrated while meditating one-pointedly and unwaveringly. Hereby you will not succumb to dullness or lethargy but will continue on the path.

When feeling agitated, direct the attention on the place below the navel, remain focused and concentrated, and meditate unwaveringly. Through this you become completely one-pointed and will not fall prey to the faults of agitation or diffusion.

In general, if your attention is one-pointed and utterly collected you cannot possibly become dull or agitated.

Now, to utilize what is beneficial for samadhi as path. The good samadhi of bliss, clarity or nonthought; feelings of loving kindness, compassion or renunciation, or strong, clear devotion — all have an experience of ensuing 'taste' accompanied by physical and verbal elaborations. These experiences are prana, which moves through the mouth. There is the danger of falling prey to ego-clinging, so it is vital to embrace them with the key point. With the attitude of understanding that they are temporary experiences dependently arising out of dualistic mind, look into the essence of each. Remain in the continuity of that without fixating on difficulty and without attachment. Then these experiences dawn as the essence of nondual wakefulness. Sustain that continuity without clinging to or nurturing the temporary experiences.

If you feel an experience of exhilaration, that attachment is abruptly cut. If you feel like weeping because of the strong compassion welling up within you, understand that the key point of the view is to recognize awareness. Don't indulge in experiencing its taste, but simply maintain in continuity.

The experience could possibly be a magical display of the *gyalpo* spirit. So that you do not wallow in nurturing a magical spirit, I shall teach you the pith instructions regarding using harmful experiences as helpers for samadhi.

No matter what happens — sickness, pain, heartache, or intense fatigue — understand it to be a temporary experience. Don't be disheartened or regard it as a misfortune. Allow the perceived object and the perceiving mind to naturally occur and be liberated. Don't regard them as faults or virtues, but let them spontaneously arise and be freed by themselves.

Now I will explain how to enhance these experiences so that they transcend help and harm. Within the all-ground, the phenomena of samsara and nirvana remain spontaneously present in the form of seeds. In the vajra body they remain as the nadi-letters and the prana-mind. Consequently, when you recognize the natural face of the true state and practice while applying the key points of samadhi, the nadi-knots are untied, the prana-mind cleared, the habitual tendencies purified, and you capture the beginning of enlightened qualities. Thus, a variety of experiences of samsara and nirvana arise.

If the pranas find an opening, they will enter. If you form a concept, the maras will manifest. If you abandon the experiences with indifference, they won't become part of the path. Understand that all these occurrences are temporary experiences.

Don't regard anything as a fault. Don't see anything as a virtue. Free from hope, fear, and doubt, train in letting the temporary experience arise naturally and be naturally liberated. In this way all experiences become enhancements.

At times when practicing in retreat, the mind is pliable, there is progress in spiritual practice and the meditator bursts into long melodious song. At other times the mind is untamable, the spiritual practice wanes, the attention scatters, and the meditator feels acutely miserable.

A variety of high and low experiences arise at the time of separating samsara and nirvana. Rather than feeling discouraged or conceited, keep to the key point of letting things spontaneously happen without attachment; thus you will be able to bring them onto the path.

Perform your retreat practice unflaggingly and without straying into distraction; then everything will be an enhancement.

Second, for clearing the hindrance of bodily sickness and pain there are five points: the basis where the sickness abides, the cause for the sickness to occur, the circumstances that activate it, its matured results, and the way to cure it.

First, sickness abides latently in the all-ground, in the manner of the constitution of the channels and as habitual tendencies. It occurs due to unwholesome karma accumulated through ignorance and ego-clinging. It is activated by means of the disturbing emotions, conceptual thinking, prana-winds, or gods and demons. Its matured results are the 404 types of disease, headed by heat and cold, phlegm, aches, and swelling. In short, the disease of coemergent ignorance is the chief cause and the disease of conceptual ignorance is the chief circumstance.

All sickness possesses these five factors: the latent basis, unwholesome karma as the cause, disturbing emotions as the circumstance, conceptual thinking as the connecting link, prana-wind as the concluding assembler, and gods and demons as the supportive factor.

For instance, if a 'coldness' disease manifests, it is caused by the habitual tendency for desire lying present in the all-ground, and is activated by the circumstance of intense desire. The connecting link is made by the conceptual thought, "I am sick! I am disabled! What shall I do if it gets worse?" This causes the 'downward clearing wind' to malfunction, opening you up to attack from the female class of evil influences.

Similarly, the seed of anger as the cause is activated through the circumstance of intense anger connected with the link of conceptual thinking. This causes the fire-equalizing wind to malfunction, opening you up to attack from the male class of evil influences, resulting in the heat diseases.

The seed of stupidity as the cause is activated by the circumstance of strong stupidity, connected with the link of conceptual thinking. This causes the 'equal-abiding wind' to malfunction, opening you up to attack from evil 'earth spirits'. It results in the phlegm diseases.

The seed of envy as the cause is activated by the circumstance of strong jealousy, connected with the link of conceptual thinking. It causes the 'life-upholding wind' to malfunction, opening you up to attack from the *tsen* class of evil influences, and resulting in the aching diseases.

The seed of pride as the cause is activated by the circumstance of strong conceit, connected with the link of conceptual thinking. It causes the 'pervading wind' to malfunction, opening you up for attack by the *gyalpo* class of evil influences and resulting in the swelling diseases.

Since the cause is ignorance, you must recognize coemergent wisdom to cure these diseases. Since the condition is disturbing emotions, you must settle your attention in evenness. Since the connector is conceptual thinking, you must cut through the ties of thought. Since the gatherer of the conclusion is wind, you must focus on the key point of wind. The back-support is the gods and demons: you must abandon the notion of a demon. By doing this you will be freed from all kinds of disease.

To cure the essence of illness there are three points: best is to leave it to be self-liberated; next-best is to abandon reference-points concerning exorcism or meditation; last is to cure it by means of visualization.

For the first, don't even take one single dose of medicine. Don't chant one syllable of a healing ceremony. Don't regard the illness as a fault, or see it as a virtue. Leave your mind unfabricated and spontaneous. Totally let be in the natural thoughtfree state of simplicity. By doing so, the flow of conceptual thinking is cut; thoughtfree wakefulness dawns, and the illness is cleared away. The sickness and the thought are liberated simultaneously.

That is to say, during the preliminaries, don't pursue the sickness. During the main part, don't cultivate the sickness. During the conclusion, don't dwell on feeling sick. Through that, you will untie old sickness and remain unharmed by new ones.

For the second, exorcising or meditating, there are three parts: transmuting adversity, cutting directly, and equalizing.

For the first, regard the sickness with gratitude, thinking again and again, "How wonderful that by means of you, sickness, I can cut through the conceptual demon!" Let your mind be jubilant; eat food that harms the illness and act in adverse ways towards it.

Next, eat some fresh 'solid fragrance,' still warm but not steaming. Drink some warm reeking 'liquid fragrance.' By meditating on the prana-wind, the disease in the upper part of the body is vomited out, and the disease in the lower part is purged out. This process of the illness vacating is the medicine of cutting through.

Second, for cutting directly, bring forth a radiant facial expression and stop whimpering. Mentally, directly cut through the worries, hopes and fears of thinking "When I am sick and weak, or if I die, what shall I do?" With total disregard, cast these worries far away.

Third, to equalize, you must utilize misfortune as your path as soon as it arises. Brighten your awareness and remind yourself of spiritual practice. Don't meditate on a visualization to counteract the illness, and don't apply any healing ritual or medical cure, but look into the identity of who feels sick! By resting in that continuous state, when an experience occurs, it vanishes by itself, and when realization occurs, it dawns as empty cognizance. At least you will not have to suffer with the thought of feeling sick.

Lastly, for curing by means of visualization, generate bodhichitta, assume the cross-legged position and visualize yourself as the yidam deity. Imagine a dark blue HUNG in your heart center, the size of a barley grain. If it is a heat disease, imagine that a white HUNG the size of a barley grain emerges from the HUNG in your heart center and circles throughout the upper part of your torso. It completely draws out all the sickness, just like a magnet collecting needles. Emerging from the top of your head it vanishes into space. Imagining this, draw the winds upward.

If it is a 'coldness' disease, imagine a red HUNG the size of a barley grain appearing from the HUNG in the heart center and circling throughout the lower part of your body. Emerging through the lower opening, imagine that it disappears into the center of the earth.

If you suffer sickness in your arms and legs such as boils or swelling, visualize a black HUNG at the location of the disease. Imagine that it gathers up the sickness and leaves through the boil or out through your fingertips.

For diseases that have not been diagnosed, imagine that a dark blue HUNG appears from the HUNG in your heart center. It gathers all the sickness throughout your body and vanishes into midair after emerging through whichever nostril the breath moves.

In general, when resting in equanimity your mind should completely become the essence of nonthought. You must cast all concerns far away and be free from doubt and hesitation about what is exorcised or visualized. The visualization and your mind should become unified. It is important to rely and concentrate upon these three points.

Here is how to dispel the hindrance of a mentality that harbors thoughts of gods and demons. When you have frequent experiences, due to the link between the structuring of your channels and the shifting of the thought flow,[17] you will be attacked by the magical displays of so-called demonic forces and feel doubt. When thoughts of fear and dread arise, identify them quickly and bring them onto the path. If you let them run wild or fall under their power, they will become an obstacle for your practice.

Moreover, unless you put any kind of hindrance, high or low, to use as your path, it will return with developed force and become an obstacle to your practice. It is essential to use hindrances as the path.

Basically, to cross the dangerous defile of your own thinking is to bring hindrances onto the path. The experiences of evil forces and magical displays are experienced within your own mistaken mind. There are definitely no 'gods' or 'demons' outside of yourself. The very moment you experience evil forces and magical displays, apply the vital point of understanding that they do not possess any true existence as they are devoid of arising, dwelling and ceasing. Whenever a magical attack occurs, assume your yogic posture, keep the gaze and look into its identity. The thought then dawns as empty cognizance. As soon as your thinking turns into empty cognizance, you possess the confident courage that thoroughly cuts through fear and dread.

Even if the hordes of Mara surround you like an army, they will not be able to move one hair on your body; nor will they be able to create any obstacles. Keep the self-assurance of thinking, "I cannot be harmed by obstacles!" To faintheartedly think "I wonder if I will meet with some obstacles!" merely creates a welcome for demons.

All experiences of gods and demons are just your own conceptual thinking taking form. They do not possess even an atom of existence outside [your own mind]. Cut the stream of conceptual thinking! Offer your aggregates as a feast offering! Give your body away as food! Cast away ego-clinging! Apply the vital point and practice!

Now, as to how to dispel the hindrance of sudden defilements (*drib*): you become defiled from meeting with or sharing food with companions who have violated their samayas, broken their precepts, or committed evil deeds; from having contact with lepers, someone whose spouse has just died, or demonic-minded people; or from staying in a house of evil deeds, demons, enmity, or moral defilement. You become befouled when eating food acquired through enmity, moral defilement, or evil deeds. Your body then becomes diseased, your samadhi weakens, and the Dharma protectors are displeased.

The sign that your samayas and precepts have been damaged is to dream that you are falling or traveling downhill. When befouled by companions, you dream of beings tainted by the dirt of other people. When befouled by a dwelling place, you dream of entering a dirty room. When befouled by food, you dream that you are eating dirt.

The best way to cure this is by means of empowerment and sadhana; the next-best by dharani mantras; and the third-best by cleansing rituals. By all means, try your best to remove defilement.

Again [Yeshe Tsogyal] asked: Pay heed to me, great master! How should a yogic practitioner bring forth enhancement through dispelling the hindrances from the path?

The master replied: Tsogyal, bringing forth enhancement on the path has three points: removing the faults that prevent enhancement, laying the basis for enhancement, and endeavoring in the methods for enhancement to occur.

First, the root of faults is nothing other than your ego-clinging, the attitude of deluded fixation, so cut the ties of ego-clinging! Cast away the fixation on enemy and friend! Forsake worldly concerns! Abandon materialistic pursuits! Engage in nothing but the Dharma from the core of your heart!

Just as a seedling doesn't grow on a stone, there will be no enhancement without removing the fault of ego-clinging. You should therefore abandon the root of all evils, ego-clinging.

Second, for laying the basis for enhancement, persevere in whichever path you have entered and exert yourself in manifesting some qualities. Engaging in numerous practices without training in one will not bring success. Understand the key point of engaging in and turning away from the path: engage in whatever [path] you have experience and turn away from other practices! Concentrate wholeheartedly until you become established in that practice. You cannot grasp for a higher path without depending upon the one below. By training like this, just like planting healthy seeds in fertile soil, you will gain experience, see your essence, and progress. In short, intensive training is the basis for qualities to arise.

Third, regarding bringing forth enhancement, there are two points: enhancing the particular path you are on, and enhancing the newly arisen experience and realization.

If you don't make any progress while practicing a teaching on means (*upaya*), the means have become one-sided due to clinging to concreteness and attributes. Bring forth enhancement by knowledge (*prajna*), understanding that all phenomena are devoid of self-nature.

If you don't make progress while practicing a teaching on knowledge (*prajna*), the knowledge has become a shortcoming due to your one-sided clinging to emptiness. Focus on the vital point of cause and effect and bring forth enhancement through the teachings on skillful means (*upaya*).

In the same way, to not progress while practicing shamatha is due to the fault of not understanding the natural state. Bring forth enhancement by means of vipashyana, the recognition of the true state.

Not to progress while practicing vipashyana is due to the shortcoming of too-brief a period of stillness. Bring forth enhancement by means of steady mindfulness and shamatha. Likewise, understand this same principle with all types of meditation and post-meditation states.

This is the key point for bringing forth enhancement in all types of daily practice.

Second, for enhancing the newly arisen [experience and realization], there is enhancement through disturbing emotions and enhancement through conceptual thinking.

For the first, there isn't anyone who doesn't have disturbing emotions, but if you stray into solid grasping, the emotions will not become part of the path. You must recognize them and utilize them as path. For this there are three points: the shortcomings of failing to do so, the good qualities of doing so, and the way to do it.

Seeing some beautiful human or nonhuman being, your mind is overtaken [with desire]. The shortcomings are that as desire increases, you create negative karma, catch the cold sicknesses, get attacked by evil female *dön* forces, and will in the future be conceived in the womb. Thus you will certainly be subject to karmic causation.

The good qualities are that you can magnetize humans and nonhumans as you wish, give rise to the samadhi of blissful emptiness, be freed from the cold sicknesses, be accompanied by the female classes of guardians, and eventually take rebirth in Sukhavati.

When you feel strong desire, it can be utilized as path in that very sitting, within that same session. Don't throw your stone at the pig's nose![18] Clean the butter lamp while it's still warm! Kill your enemy when you catch him!

First, let the desire grow to its full strength. Then, before creating any karma, bring it onto the path. Since it is your own mind that solidifies the fixation of desire, when the identity of this attitude dawns as unformed wakefulness, the auspicious coincidence is fully formed. Without this basis of original wakefulness, desire doesn't become the path, just as a reflection is not seen unless the mirror is free from dirt. The strength of the disturbing emotion is fully developed. When the emotion is experienced within the state of original wakefulness, no karma is created. It is brought onto the path without interrupting it with any other thought, just like the analogy of the philosopher's stone.

The actual way of bringing it onto the path is for you to look into the identity of the desire and let be within the natural state. Its identity then vividly dawns as naked nonconceptual wakefulness in which bliss and emptiness are nondual.

Additionally, while you train like this, bring desire onto the path by means of loving kindness, compassion, and bodhichitta. First, generate the enlightened attitude; next, be free of mental constructs; and lastly, seal by dedication. By generating bodhichitta, your emotion becomes the path of enlightenment. By letting be in a state free of constructs, realization arises. And by sealing with dedication, the virtue is perfected.

Train undistractedly in this way with each thought state, from the moment it arises until it has been brought onto the path. Do not be interrupted by other thoughts between the acts of generating bodhichitta to sealing with dedication: if you do, it doesn't become the path.

It is the same key point in the case of the other emotions such as feeling angry, dull, proud, or jealous. Bring them undistractedly onto the path; then allow the identity to dawn as original wakefulness. Let them develop to full strength without creating any karmic actions.

Second, regarding enhancement through conceptual thinking, there are two parts: good thoughts and bad thoughts. The first type is when you have a temporary "good experience" of excited states of mind, receive a prophecy of a deity, or have eminent signs of auspiciousness. You then regard these occurrences as something excellent, consider their good qualities, and savor their taste. If you try to improve the experience, it vanishes. If you remain indifferent towards it, there is no enhancement.

To bring forth enhancement, don't indulge in a "good" thought state, don't cling to it as being a good quality, and don't savor its taste. What you regard as "goodness" only comes from your mind. Using the method explained above, bring it onto the path without being distracted by other thoughts, until the identity of mind dawns as original wakefulness.

The other type involves unwanted experiences, mental turmoil, or a magical attack of demons. Generally you regard these occurrences as something negative, consider them to be faults, and savor their taste: by doing this, they turn into obstacles. Don't reject bad thoughts, don't regard them as disadvantages, don't indulge in them. "Badness" is just the magical creation of your mind. Bring it onto the path as described above, until their identity dawns as original wakefulness.

The topics up to this point were the complete necessities for the path of a yogi.

Now, regarding the fruition of having perfected the path, there are four points. The first is the way of acting for the welfare of beings; the second is the way the wisdom mind remains; the third is the way of seeing those to be tamed through compassion; and the fourth is a refutation of other people's incorrect ideas.

First, when the defilements that obscure the path are purified, you have realized the innate and originally awakened state. This has four aspects: meaning, sign, identity, and way of manifestation. The five kayas that are the foundation; the five ways of speech that communicate understanding; the five ways of mind that are nonconceptual; the five qualities that fulfill needs; and the five activities that function for the welfare of others.

First are the five kayas. Dharmakaya is nonarising, pure and unconfined, and functions as the basis for the four wisdom kayas. Sambhogakaya is original wakefulness of perfect (*sam*) qualities that enjoys (*bhoga*), without fixating, the multiplicity of phenomena. It functions as the basis for *nirmana*-apparitions. Nirmanakaya magically appears (*nirmana*) in accordance with the mentality of those to be tamed, without departing from dharmakaya. It functions as the basis for the wisdom qualities that are displayed in whatever way necessary for those who need to be tamed. *Vajrakaya* is original wakefulness, the indivisible emptiness and awareness which demonstrates thatness. *Abhisambodhikaya* is undivided fearlessness, permanent in essence. It spontaneously cognizes all phenomena as an locationless, original wakefulness that is naturally aware.

Second are the five ways of speech. The ultimate speech of dharmakaya, the expressed, is utterly pure wakefulness that forms the basis for all thought and expression. The intended symbolic speech of sambhogakaya is original wakefulness communicating meaning by the sight of the bodily form. The verbal speech of nirmanakaya is original wakefulness that communicates with the six classes of beings by means of the sixty aspects of melodious voice. It gives understanding to the meaning of each word within the experience of those to be tamed. The speech of vajra wisdom is original wakefulness that communicates understanding of nondual audible emptiness. The *abhisambodhi* speech of naturally cognizant awareness is original wakefulness that cognizes all sound as being awareness and which illuminates meaning through blessings endowed with the fivefold wisdom of mind.

Third are the five ways of awakened mind. The mind of great bliss is the nonconceptual wakefulness of the empty innate nature. The mind of nonthought is original wakefulness that cognizes yet doesn't conceptualize phenomena. The mind of equality is the original wakefulness of the nonduality of all phenomena. Vajra mind is the original wakefulness in which all phenomena are undivided appearance and emptiness. The mind that liberates beings functions for the welfare of beings by means of the four activities of nonattachment.

Fourth, the five qualities are the realm, palace, light rays, throne, and ornaments. The dharmakaya realm is the naturally pure space of dharmadhatu.

The sambhogakaya realm is the 'light-wheel' of natural radiance. The nirmana-kaya realm is the billionfold *Saha world*.

The palace for dharmakaya is the dharmadhatu of *Akanishtha*; for sambho-gakaya it is the original wakefulness of individual experience; and for nirmana-kaya it is the mandala arising from individual experience.

The light rays for dharmakaya are the light rays of the five wisdoms. For sambhogakaya they are the natural radiance of wisdom that shines with five-colored light. It is taught that nirmanakaya has 60 billion rays of light shining from each portion of the body.

The throne for dharmakaya is the throne of the unified view; for sambho-gakaya it is unified knowledge; and for nirmanakaya it is unified compassion.

As for ornaments, dharmakaya has the ornament of nonarising purity. Sambhogakaya has the ornaments of unceasing natural cognizance, the extraor-dinary major and minor marks, and the ten symbolic ornaments: crown, ear-rings, choker and short necklace, arm-rings, two bracelets and two anklets, and the long necklace. The nirmanakaya ornaments are the general 32 major and 80 minor marks. The qualities of the vajrakaya and abhisambodhikaya are not mentioned.

The five activities are: pacifying karma and disturbing emotions; increasing life-span, merit and naturally aware wisdom; magnetizing mind, awareness, and all the phenomena of samsara and nirvana; eliminating everything that is not conducive; and the direct action that realizes the natural state.

Now, about the way of acting for the welfare of beings, there are three as-pects: acting with a support, acting without a support, and acting by nature.

Acting with a support means to function for the welfare of pure beings through sambhogakaya and for impure beings through nirmanakaya with the nondual wakefulness of dharmakaya as the basis. This is the way of stating that wisdom is present.

Acting without a support means to function for the welfare of beings by appearing as the two rupakayas within the perception of those to be tamed, even though the awakened state of buddhahood has no wisdom comprised of a solid individual being. This is the way of stating that wisdom is absent.

Acting for the welfare of beings by nature means functioning through the expression of the innate nature of all things that is "no thing" whatsoever and yet manifests in every way possible. This is the way of nonduality [of the two ways above].

To explain further, the 'doer' is the spontaneously present five kayas called Vajradhara. These five kayas are just subdivisions of qualities; they are not five concrete, separate entities. The vajrakaya and abhisambodhikaya are names for aspects of the three kayas, while dharmakaya, sambhogakaya and nirmanakaya are the actual kayas.

The dharmakaya, being the aspect of realization for the benefit of self, does not act for the welfare of beings. But the two rupakayas do function for the benefit of others. This means that sambhogakaya acts for the welfare of pure beings such as the *bodhisattvas* of the ten bhumis, while the nirmanakaya acts for the welfare of the six classes of impure beings.

Functioning altruistically in inconceivable ways are the bases of the twelve deeds of dharmakaya, the six superknowledges of mind, and the four inconceivables. The ways of functioning, when subdivided are the twelve aspects of supreme speech; when condensed, they are the three collections of the Tripitaka; when considering the remedies, they are the mending-purification; and when considering cause and effect, they are the vehicles of Mantra and Philosophy.

The sugatas remain as the basic state of wisdom mind which is the indivisibility of the *two truths*, without falling into any extreme whatsoever, and free from being identical or different. The ultimate fruition is to realize and remain in original wakefulness indivisible from the omniscient wisdom mind of the awakened ones, without dwelling in any extreme whatsoever, free from being singular or plural, and beyond being identical or different.

This basic state of wisdom mind is free from being singular, since the 25 attributes of fruition manifest from the aspects of Samantabhadra's qualities. It is free from being plural, since this manifestation of the 25 attributes of fruition are contained within the single self-existing wakefulness of Samantabhadra's mind. Moreover, [wisdom mind] is free from being singular because it appears as the buddhas of the three kayas within the perception of those to be tamed. Also, it is free from being plural because they are real, substantial entities, but are one in being empty and devoid of self.

If wisdom mind was really singular, the transformation of the thought states would be false; if it was truly different entities, a single buddha would not manifest in multiple emanations. It therefore abides free from being either identical or different.

The way of seeing those to be tamed and the refutation of incorrect ideas is as follows. That which is seen are the dispositions of the sentient beings to be tamed. That which sees is the compassion of the teaching Buddha. The way of seeing is threefold: the wisdom of knowing [the nature of things] as it is sees that all phenomena do not arise. The wisdom of knowing all that exists sees that all phenomena do not cease. The wisdom of knowing nonduality sees that all phenomena are nondual.

I shall now refute other people's incorrect ideas.[19] Consider this: do the objects seen, the appearances of the dispositions of sentient beings, exist in a buddha's experience? If they do exist, these confused experiences must be real entities because they appear within true experience. Consequently, they must ultimately be false. If they don't, then a buddha's perception must be incorrect because of seeing something to be what it isn't. This would be like the eye consciousness that apprehends two moons because of seeing solidly existing entities.[20] Since this doesn't necessarily follow, the two truths are consequently indivisible.

Emaho!
This is the secret, unexcelled cycle of the supreme vehicle,
The true essence of the definitive meaning,
The short path for attaining buddhahood in one life.
After connecting with this, you who follow my advice
Are fortunate ones, the heart children of Uddiyana!

This Treasury of Precious Jewels to Remove Hindrances
Is an essential and radiant lamp, that like the light
Of the sun and moon, illuminates the completion stage.
In a future time a destined hidden yogi
Will meet with these pith instructions,
So, Tsogyal, conceal them as a terma treasure!

Twelve *Tenma Goddesses*, guard this teaching!
Six hundred and thirty years from now,
A destined man of the wrathful type who masters termas,
Will appear from the eastern direction; entrust it to him!

When this destined person connects with these instructions,
He should not reveal them wantonly, but should teach only after
examining who is worthy.

Thus he spoke.

Lady Tsogyal concealed this within the white treasury of conch on the slope of the northern mountainside that resembles a heap of poisonous snakes.

This was revealed by Rigdzin Gökyi Demtru Chen, the vidyadhara with the vulture feather, from within the white treasury of conch on the slope of the mountainside that resembles a heap of poisonous snakes.

Samaya, seal, seal, seal.

ADVICE ON HOW TO PRACTICE THE DHARMA CORRECTLY:

꧁꧂

PADMAKARA, THE MASTER OF UDDIYANA, resided at Samye after being invited to Tibet by the king. He gave numerous teachings to the king, his chieftains, and other devoted people in the eastern part of the central temple. Since they didn't understand correctly, he gave this advice repeatedly.

Master Padma said: No matter how much I teach, the people of Tibet don't understand; instead they engage in nothing other than perverted actions. If you want to practice the Dharma from the core of your heart, do like this:

To be a Buddhist lay person (*upasaka*) doesn't just mean to observe the four root precepts; it means to cast unvirtuous misdeeds far away. To be a novice (*shramana*) doesn't merely mean to assume a pure exterior; it means to practice virtue correctly. To be a monk (*bhikshu*) doesn't only mean to control body, speech, and mind in daily activities and to be forbidden to do all kinds of things; it means to bring all roots of virtue to the path of great enlightenment.

To be virtuous doesn't simply mean to wear yellow robes; it means to fear the ripening of karma. To be a spiritual friend doesn't just mean to assume a dignified demeanor; it means to be the glorious protector of everyone. To be a yogi doesn't merely mean to behave crudely; it means to mingle one's mind with the nature of dharmata.

To be a *mantrika* doesn't just mean to mutter incantations [with a malevolent attitude]; it means to swiftly attain enlightenment through the path of uniting means and knowledge. To be a meditator doesn't simply mean to live in a cave; it means to train oneself in the true meaning [of the natural state]. To be a hermit doesn't just mean to live in the deep forest; it means that one's mind is free from dualistic constructs.

To be learned doesn't only mean to uphold the eight worldly concerns; it means to distinguish between right and wrong.[21] To be a bodhisattva doesn't mean to retain self-interest within; it means to exert oneself in the means of liberating all sentient beings from samsara.

To have faith doesn't mean to whimper; it means to enter the right path out of fear of death and rebirth. To be diligent doesn't mean to engage in various restless activities; it means to exert oneself in the means of leaving samsaric existence behind. To be generous doesn't merely mean to give with bias and partiality; it means to be profoundly free from attachment to anything whatsoever.

Oral instruction doesn't mean many written books; it means a few words that strike the vital point of meaning in your mind. View doesn't simply mean philosophical opinion; it means to be free from the limitations of mental constructs. Meditation doesn't mean to fixate on something with thought; it means your mind is stable in natural cognizance, free from fixation.

Spontaneous action doesn't just mean to act with crazy abandon; it means to be free from fixation on deluded perceptions as being real. Discriminating knowledge (*prajna*) doesn't mean the sharp intellect of mistaken thought; it means to understand that all phenomena are nonarising and devoid of mental constructs.

Learning doesn't just mean to receive teachings through one's ears; it means to cut through misconceptions and have realization beyond conceptual mind. Reflecting doesn't only mean to pursue conceptual thinking and form assumptions; it means to cut through your deluded clinging. Fruition doesn't only mean the rupakayas invited down from Akanishtha; it means to recognize the nature of mind and attain stability in that.

Don't mistake mere words to be the meaning of the teachings. Mingle the practice with your own being and attain liberation from samsara right now.

POINTING THE STAFF AT THE OLD MAN:

﷽

WHILE THE GREAT MASTER PADMASAMBHAVA was staying in Great Rock Hermitage at Samye, Sherab Gyalpo of Ngog, an uneducated 61 year old man who had the highest faith and strong devotion to the master, served him for one year. All this while Ngog didn't ask for any teachings, nor did the master give him any. When after a year the master intended to leave, Ngog offered a mandala plate upon which he placed a flower of one ounce of gold. Then he said, "Great master, think of me with kindness. First of all, I am uneducated. Second, my intelligence is small. Third, I am old, so my elements are worn down. I beg you to give a teaching to an old man on the verge of death that is simple to understand, can thoroughly cut through doubt, is easy to realize and apply, has an effective view, and will help me in future lives."

The master pointed his walking staff at the old man's heart and gave this instruction: Listen here, old man! Look into the awakened mind of your own awareness! It has neither form nor color, neither center nor edge. At first, it has no origin but is empty. Next, it has no dwelling place but is empty. At the end, it has no destination but is empty. This emptiness is not made of anything and is clear and cognizant. When you see this and recognize it, you know your natural face. You understand the nature of things. You have then seen the nature of mind, resolved the basic state of reality and cut through doubts about topics of knowledge.

This awakened mind of awareness is not made out of any material substance; it is self-existing and inherent in yourself. This is the nature of things that is easy to realize because it is not to be sought for elsewhere. This is the nature of mind that does not consist of a concrete perceiver and something perceived to fixate on. It defies the limitations of permanence and annihilation. In it there is no thing to awaken; the awakened state of enlightenment is your own awareness that is naturally awake. In it there is no thing that goes to the hells; awareness is naturally pure. In it there is no practice to carry out; its nature is naturally cognizant. This great view of the natural state is present in yourself: resolve that it is not to be sought for elsewhere.

When you understand the view in this way and want to apply it in your experience, wherever you stay is the mountain retreat of your body. Whatever external appearance you perceive is a naturally occurring appearance and a naturally empty emptiness; let it be, free from mental constructs. Naturally freed appearances become your helpers, and you can practice while taking appearances as the path.

Within, whatever moves in your mind, whatever you think, has no essence but is empty. Thought occurrences are naturally freed. When remembering your mind essence you can take thoughts as the path and the practice is easy.

As for the innermost advice: no matter what kind of disturbing emotion you feel, look into the emotion and it tracelessly subsides. The disturbing emotion is thus naturally freed. This is simple to practice.

When you can practice in this way, your meditation training is not confined to sessions. Knowing that everything is a helper, your meditation experience is unchanging, the innate nature is unceasing, and your conduct is unshackled. Wherever you stay, you are never apart from the innate nature.

Once you realize this, your material body may be old, but awakened mind doesn't age. It knows no difference between young and old. The innate nature is beyond bias and partiality. When you recognize that awareness, innate wakefulness, is present in yourself, there is no difference between sharp and dull faculties. When you understand that the innate nature, free from bias and partiality, is present in yourself, there is no difference between great and small learning. Even though your body, the support for the mind, falls apart, the dharmakaya of awareness wisdom is unceasing. When you gain stability in this unchanging state, there is no difference between a long or short life-span.

Old man, practice the true meaning! Take the practice to heart! Don't mistake words and meaning! Don't part from your friend, diligence! Embrace everything with mindfulness! Don't indulge in idle talk and pointless gossip! Don't become involved in common aims! Don't disturb yourself with the worry of offspring! Don't excessively crave food and drink! Intend to die an ordinary man![22] Your life is running out, so be diligent! Practice this instruction for an old man on the verge of death!"

Because of pointing the staff at Sherab Gyalpo's heart, this is called 'The Instruction of Pointing the Staff at the Old Man.' Sherab Gyalpo of Ngog was liberated and attained accomplishment.

This was written down by the Princess of Kharchen for the sake of future generations. It is known under the name 'The Instruction of Pointing the Staff.'

ORAL ADVICE ON PRACTICE:

❧

NAMO GURU DEVA DAKINI HUNG

THE GREAT MASTER PADMAKARA, who upholds the life-pillar of the words of all the buddhas, helped the people of Tibet enter the door of the Dharma. Although they wished to take refuge in the Three Jewels, they didn't know how to direct their minds towards practice. When misfortune such as sickness befell them, they cowardly resorted to divination, shamanistic incantation, and astrology. Padmakara therefore gave them this oral advice on practice. Tibetan practitioners of the degenerate age, take this to heart!

In order to make your spiritual practice meaningful, apply it whenever you need a remedy. If you have a horrible experience, keep the Three Jewels, the objects of refuge, in mind! In all daily activities such as walking, moving about, lying down or sitting, remember your master at the crown of your head! To part with bodhichitta causes the root of the Mahayana to rot, so never separate yourself from arousing the mind set on supreme enlightenment!

To feel stingy when giving alms causes rebirth as a hungry ghost, so don't stray into miserliness even when giving away the smallest thing! To give rise to desire while keeping the vows of chastity causes rebirth in the hell of putrid corpses, so don't cultivate lust for intercourse! To get angry while training in patience and bodhichitta causes the agonizing experience of being burned

104

amidst a blazing furnace within an iron box, so never part from the armor of patience!

If you slip into laziness when trying to accomplish unexcelled enlightenment, keep in mind that your life runs out without lingering even an instant, so don't fall prey to indolence! Your life-span slips away as night follows day: keep that in mind!

When adhering to a scheduled spiritual practice, it is of utmost importance to dedicate the merit of observing the precepts six times during day and night! Sleeping like an ordinary corpse is more base than a cow! Not to practice the Dharma after having obtained a human body is more vile than being a festering leper! Not to fear the ripening of karma while knowing about good and evil actions is equivalent to insanity! Realize that even a minor infraction can ripen into a mountain of suffering. Keep that in mind!

It is of utmost important to cherish even the smallest virtuous action like you would your own heart! To take the life of another is no different from murdering your own parents or children! To feel desire upon seeing a woman causes rebirth as a microbe in the womb, so apply the remedy of renunciation! To intend to take what belongs to another without it being given causes you to be born in poverty and want for many aeons. Beware of the miseries of involving yourself with farm work, farm animals and employees in this lifetime!

You needn't discourage yourself by thinking, "How can someone with karma like mine practice the Dharma?" Even the blessed Buddha Shakyamuni was once Nangje, the son of a potter! Don't feel proud or inflated with self-conceit about some superficial virtue you may have. All the buddhas are not conceited, even though their omniscience and qualities are beyond measure!

When meeting misfortune, if you do not place your trust in the Three Jewels but instead resort to shamanistic healing rituals and taking refuge in mundane spirits, that is a sign that you have given rise to wrong views about the teachings of the Greater Vehicle. Don't be an embarrassment to the Buddha's teachings!

Whenever you suffer misfortune or illness, think "This repays my karmic debts from former lifetimes and purifies my negative karma!" No matter what happiness you have, regard it as the kindness of the Three Jewels and arouse the strong yearning of devoted gratitude! When you meet with enmity and hatred, think "This is a good friend helping me to cultivate patience!" Think, "This helper for patience is a messenger sent by the victorious ones!"

When your friends and relatives show love and affection they are the fetters of samsara, so think, "These fetters are the obstacles sent by Mara to prevent me from accomplishing unexcelled enlightenment!" Think also, "All sentient beings of the three realms are my own parents. What a pity that my parents wander in samsara! But it is not enough to just pity them: with the four immeasurables and by various other means, I must guide them out of samsara until samsara is empty!" Keep that in mind!

No matter what enjoyment and distraction you encounter during this lifetime, think: "This is the seduction of Mara to prevent me from attaining unexcelled enlightenment! This Mara is more dreadful than a poisonous viper!" Keep that in mind! Although you may have perfect conditions in this life, they are just fleeting, futile and momentary. Keep that in mind!

Whatever attainments you apply yourself to in this world are only fleeting, and will torment you with deluded disturbance. Keep that in mind! Exert yourself in turning away from this delusion! It is certain that you must depart while leaving behind your entire kingdom, desirable objects and possessions! Nothing besides the Dharma will help you at that time. Keep that in mind!23

Now you must seek a good companion for the time of departure. That is most important! Keep that in mind! As for this companion, it is essential in this life to keep company with whomever or whatever helps you to attain unexcelled enlightenment. Keep that in mind! When you meet with misfortune, understand that this is the teacher who exhorts you to virtue and that this teacher is most kind! Keep that in mind!

When your body meets severe illness, think, "This is a whip to drive me to proceed on the path of enlightenment. This is the object of refuge leading me on the path." This temporary body will at some point be left behind as an ordinary corpse. There is no way to avoid that! When clinging to this aggregation of flesh and blood as being oneself, think, "This is an evil spirit who has entered my heart!" Without distraction, do whatever you can to expel this evil spirit! The experiences of this life are devoid of a self-nature, just like dreams and magic. Keep that in mind!

You and all others are deluded by not recognizing what is devoid of a self-nature to be so. This delusion must be immediately sent back into dharmata. Keep that in mind! Not doing that will cause you to wander endlessly in samsara and to undergo unbearable suffering. Give up all other activities and exert yourself in nothing other than Dharma practice which will enable you to accomplish unexcelled enlightenment. This is the most important! As for this Dharma practice, it is not enough to just 'have practiced.' You must apply the profound teachings correctly. Keep that in mind!

When you practice correctly in this way, the flow of samsara reverses. When this flow has been reversed, the flow of great bliss will be unceasing. Keep that in mind! Practitioners of future generations will not listen to this advice of mine. They will place their trust in divinations and shamanistic incantations and will be deceived. Keep that in mind!

When you listen carefully to this and put it correctly into practice, you will certainly automatically receive the blessings! When you assimilate loving kindness in you heart, you will be loved by all beings. When you hold compassion in your heart, everyone will cherish you as their own child. When you keep impartiality in your heart, you will be free from enmity and prejudice. When you fill your heart with sympathetic joy, your actions will be in harmony with everyone.

When you give up the thought of harming others, you will meet less hostility. When you tame your mind and are very generous, many followers will gather around you. When you relinquish jealousy and arrogance, you will be slandered less. When you give up restless activity and bustling about, you will have fewer faults.

When your mind turns away from craving, then food, wealth and enjoyments will automatically gather. When you observe the precepts purely in your being, your mind will be pliable. When you don't have any ambition or desire whatsoever, the accumulations will naturally be perfected. When you understand the characteristics of samsara, your mind will turn away from worldly pursuits.

When your mind is involved in the profound teaching of dharmata and you apply it in practice, you will meet with many misfortunes and obstacles.[24] When you keep company with an eminent master, his qualities will automatically influence you. When your devotion to the Three Jewels is unceasing, you will quickly receive the blessings.

When you study and reflect without prejudice, you will be less sectarian about the teachings and the schools of philosophy. When you practice the profound development and completion, you will have powers and blessings. When your appearance conforms with worldly conventions, you will encounter less criticism.

When you give up the fixation of attachment and clinging, your body and mind will be at ease. When you live in mountain retreats, experience will dawn. When you cast away self-cherishing and ego-clinging, you will not be harmed by the obstacles of Mara. When your mind looks into itself, dharmata will dawn from within.

When you constantly exert yourself in practice, limitless virtues will manifest. When you recognize the nature of mind, fabrication and effort are naturally freed. When you realize that samsara and nirvana are dharmakaya, you need not put effort into meditation practice. When your practice doesn't stray into laziness, you will not feel regret at the moment of death.

Fortunate ones, mingle your mind with the Dharma and the happiness of buddhahood will manifest within you!

Listen again! Unless you tame your disturbing emotions, you will have enemies and opposition: this is pointless, so let your mind rest freely!

You may try to support your family and friends, but at the time of death all other actions besides the virtuous practices of Dharma activities will have been pointless. So constantly apply yourself to spiritual practices in thought, word, and deed!

You may pursue worldly fame and gain, but unless you follow the teachings of the Buddha, such activity will only be the cause for throwing you back into further samsara. So adhere to the teachings of the Buddha!

Your castle of earth and stone may be beautiful, but unless you dwell in the fortress of the unchanging, you must depart and leave it behind. So keep to the fortress of the unchanging!

You may gather wealth and possessions, but only the two accumulations can be enjoyed after death. So gather the two accumulations as much as you can!

You may consume all kinds of delicious food, but unless you adhere to the nectar of the innate nature, it all turns into a heap of filth. So drink the nectar of the profound instructions!

You may dearly treasure this body of flesh and blood and cling to it as being yourself, but as it is only on loan from the elements, unless you attain the nonarising dharmakaya, it will soon be snatched away. So, treasure and capture the stronghold of nonarising dharmakaya!

You may consort with one thousand amiable friends, but unless you keep company with means and knowledge, you will soon be separated from them. So keep company with means and knowledge!

Your fame and renown may fill a billion universes, but unless you recognize your inconceivable and inexpressible nature, it is all only Mara's attempt to seduce you. So pursue the ineffable, inconceivable and indescribable nature!

You may possess the power and might of a world ruler, but unless you gain mastery over your own mind, when the time of death arrives you still haven't attained the power of freedom. So gain mastery over your mind!

You may have the bravery of a strong fighter, but unless you possess the intelligent strength of discriminating knowledge, you will not turn the tide in the battle with samsara. So possess the intelligent strength of discriminating knowledge!

You may speak like the Lion of Speech [Manjushri], but unless you take to heart the primordially pure nature of resounding emptiness, that will not prevent the ripening of karma. So take to heart the primordially pure nature of empty resounding!

You may ride the finest stallion, but unless you discover the great bliss within yourself, it will not let you escape the miseries of samsara. So seek the nature of great bliss!

Your body may be as magnificent as a god, but unless you adorn yourself with the superior qualities of buddhahood, it will not seduce the Demon of Death. So adorn yourself with the eminent virtues of the victorious ones!

Unless you seek protection from your master and the Three Jewels, nothing can save you from the attacks of disturbing emotions. So seek protective escort from the guru and the Three Jewels!

Unless you realize that your own mind is the buddha, you will be deceived by the multitude of conceptual thoughts. So realize that your own mind is the buddha!

In short, your numerous worldly pursuits that are not causes for liberation or omniscient enlightenment will, in addition to being futile, only cause further samsaric misery. So it is essential to exert yourself, heart and soul and in thought, word, and deed, in accomplishing the unexcelled enlightenment!

Listen once again! The reason why people don't turn their minds away from worldly pursuits is because they don't understand cause and effect and the characteristics of samsara. The cause of samsara is failing to abandon the dualistic fixation on a self-entity. Since within the awakened state of mind, self and other beings are one, people who discriminate between self and other have no sense! Since each and every being of the three realms, one after the other, have been your loving parents, people who regard others as either enemy or friend have no sense!

Since at this time we must make the separation between samsara and nirvana, people who find the time to tend to worldly pursuits have no sense! Since this life lasts only for a short while, like a sojourn in a travelers' lodge, people who busy themselves with building houses and mansions have no sense! Since this body is filled with impure substances and cannot bear even the touch of a thorn, people who cling to it as being themselves have no sense!

Since family and friends are impermanent and pass away, people who expect to live forever have no sense! Since you will have to leave empty-handed at the time of death, people who pursue food and wealth through all kinds of evil deeds have no sense! Since outer appearances change and perish, people who expect their enjoyments to last forever have no sense!

Since your life-span decreases like the shadow of the setting sun, people who are lazy and indolent have no sense! Since Dharma practice secures happiness in both this life and the future, people who turn back from it and instead engage in family life have no sense! Since it is certain that one goes to the lower realms by committing evil deeds, people who don't fear the ripening of karma have no sense!

People who are unable, at present, to bear even the touch of a spark of fire, but who expect to be able to endure the hot hells, have no sense! Those who are unable to bear even one night of winter cold but who expect to be able to endure the cold hells have no sense! People who are unable to bear even three days of hunger and thirst but who expect to be able to endure the misery of a hungry ghost have no sense! Unable to bear the hardship of carrying a load for even a short while, people who expect to be able to endure the misery of a beast of burden have no sense!

Since this is the time when one needs good advice, people who don't listen even when a master teaches have no sense! Since this is the time when one has achieved some freedom of choice, people who make themselves the slaves of sense pleasures have no sense! Neglecting to practice the Dharma for even a single moment, people who expect to enjoy abundant happiness in future lives have no sense!

Death is your innate possession as soon as you are born; people who feel at leisure to prepare for tomorrow and ignore the proximity of the time of death have no sense! Now you have the choice to go up or down; people who don't engage themselves in Dharma practices that bring liberation have no sense! Samsaric deeds only result in misery; people who don't abandon this self-created suffering have no sense! Since you wander endlessly in samsara, people who keep on deceiving themselves have no sense!

When the degenerate age of this aeon arrives, people are their own deceivers, their own bad counsel, the makers of their own stupidity, lying to and fooling themselves. How sad that these people have human forms but possess no more sense than an ox!

Listen once again! You who wish to practice the Dharma from the core of your heart, do like this: Follow your master and the Three Jewels with a devotion as constant as the flow of a river! Care for your followers, attendants and all other beings with kindness and compassion, as lovingly as a mother cares for her only child!

Gain strength and ability and liberate the enemies of the Buddhadharma: be as powerful as the thrust of a thunderbolt! Don't be lazy, but exert yourself in virtuous activities in thought, word, and deed as energetically as a vain maiden whose hair has caught fire! Be conscientious regarding good and evil, and with an attention as fine as barley flour as to the cause and effect of karmic deeds, shun nonvirtue like a poison!

Resolve to emulate the deeds of all the sublime and noble-minded forefathers and follow the example of holy beings![25] Take the gurus, yidams, dakinis, and Dharma protectors as witness to your vows, and observe your vows carefully, with good conscience! Use yourself as the yardstick of patience and don't hurt or inflict harm upon others!

Whatever you do, never depart from what is meaningful, but turn your thoughts, words, and deeds toward the Dharma! Don't criticize others; instead, expose your own faults to the world! Help faithful people to enter the Dharma in whichever way is suitable by means of teaching the expedient or definitive meaning!

All types of impermanence, such as death or separation, are messages to you, so pay heed! Don't busy yourself with many distracting activities, but relax your body and mind! Practice by applying the profound instructions to your own state of mind!

No matter how destitute you may be, don't deceitfully seek food and wealth! When your mind is filled with dread, don't be hostile to obstructing spirits! Even for the sake of a kingdom, don't cause harm to other beings!

Since the time of death lies uncertain, capture the stronghold of the nature of mind! Seek a qualified master, always venerate him at the crown of your head, and develop the yearning of faith and devotion!

Since you don't know what is needed in this life, study all the topics of knowledge!26 No matter what learning you gain, conceit gives foothold to the demon of disaster, so humble your pride!

Always keep to remote mountain dwellings, since solitude is the source of happiness! Don't live the life of an evil householder, since that causes misery for this and all future lives! Since companions influence your daily deeds, associate with people who are in harmony with the Dharma!

Until you attain realization through meditation training, don't brag or act in crude ways! Cast away prejudice and partisanship, since they are the chains of samsara! Don't be hypocritical or pretentious, because that is scorned and despised by all wise people!

Don't remain amidst ordinary people; evil behavior naturally contaminates! Don't place your trust in any conditioned phenomena; everything is a magical apparition! Gain certainty in your own mind; the awakened state is not elsewhere!

When you abandon and adopt these prescribed ways, you will uphold the teachings of Shakyamuni.

Listen once more! If you wish to practice the Dharma from the core of your heart, base your Dharma practice upon observing the precepts which are like the earth! Perfect the vehicles of philosophy within a view like the expanse of space! By distinguishing details as clearly as the colors of a rainbow, keep all the teachings in mind, distinct and unmixed!

Guide the destined ones with the correct sequence of teachings, like gradually peeling away the layered bark of a plantain tree! Nurture destined and worthy disciples with the oral instructions, as lovingly as if you were tending seedlings!

Remember the meditation training as clearly and vividly as flowers in autumn! Like a healer, take instructions from all directions and apply them whenever they are needed! Be moderate, as when using salt on your food!

Cut directly through misfortune, like a wild yak heading straight to the top of the valley! When encountering disturbing emotions, abandon them as you would your hated enemies! When their antidote, original wakefulness, has taken birth within you, protect it within your stream of being as carefully as your eyes!

When clearing misconceptions and doubt through learning and reflection, serve a master with the flexibility of a young deer! Concerning worldly affairs, be as stubborn as an old bull, not allowing anyone to lead you along by the nose! When training in the four immeasurables, equalize all with the endurance of a sheep!

If the time comes to utilize your learning through debate, cut through with intelligence that is completely unimpeded like the sword of a warrior! When seeking the meaning through reflection, tame your dullness and agitation just as you would tame a wild stallion! When assimilating experience within yourself, cast away all mundane pursuits, like a celebrity who has caught leprosy!

In short, to quickly awaken and accomplish unexcelled enlightenment, it is essential to observe yourself in all situations and control yourself in regard to cause and effect as carefully as a newly wedded bride!

Listen again! An even temper and a gentle manner of speech is necessary for facilitating the birth of loving kindness within you. Curiosity and an active mind give you the good quality of easily feeling faith. A sense of honor and modesty gives you the good quality of perseverance in Dharma practice.

Meeting suffering and misfortune gives you the good quality of turning your interest towards the Dharma. Honesty and trustworthiness imparts the good quality of being able to bear difficulty. Constancy and deep affection generate the good quality of being truly able to serve your master.

Distaste for advantage and status give you the good quality of being uninvolved in partisanship concerning the Buddhadharma. To be careless in mundane affairs gives you the good quality of greater ability in retaining the sacred Dharma. To stand by your word imparts the good quality of being in harmony with the Dharma.

To be resolute and tenacious gives you the good quality of higher excellence when practicing the Dharma. To keep a smiling face and gentle behavior gives you the good quality of pure samaya with your Dharma friends. To be unfocused and spontaneous during daily activities gives you the good quality of being able to directly cut through conceptual thinking.

On the other hand, these characteristics can become shortcomings if one is overwhelmed by them, as follows: People with an even temper and a gentle manner of speech are in danger of falling prey to the faults of pretense and dishonesty. Curious people with active minds have the fault of easily relinquishing Dharma practice. People with a sense of honor and modesty have the fault of failing to leave worldly affairs behind.

People who experience much suffering and misfortune are in danger of not finding free time even though they intend to practice the Dharma. People who are honest and trusting are in danger of falling prey to the fault of not understanding the Dharma. People who are constant and have deep affection for relatives have the fault of not cutting the ties to worldly affairs.

People with distaste for advantage and status risk falling prey to not applying the antidote in their practice of the sacred Dharma. People who are careless in mundane affairs risk failing to reach to the end of Dharma practice. People who stand by their word risk falling prey to the fault of harsh words leading to arguments and strife.

People who are resolute and tenacious risk having difficulty in abandoning ill-will. People who keep a smiling face and gentle behavior risk being overly hypocritical and fond of romance. People who are unfocused and spontaneous don't exert themselves in Dharmic activities and risk falling prey to the fault of belittling the ripening of karma.

All you who may have entered the gate to the Dharma: if you cast away all faults and make yourself possess all virtues, you will accomplish the unexcelled enlightenment without difficulty, so keep this in mind!

Listen once again! There are many people who are not in accord with the Dharma although they have entered its gate, so you must make sure it doesn't happen to you! You may have taken ordination, but you are not a Dharma practitioner if your means of livelihood and your possessions are the same as those of a householder. You may have abandoned worldly activities, but you are not a Dharma practitioner if you haven't given up ordinary idle gossip.

You may dwell in a hermitage, but you are not a Dharma practitioner if your activities are the same as that of a worldly person. You may have left your homeland behind, but you are not a Dharma practitioner if you haven't cut your ties to worldly people. You may be persevering in practice, but you are not a Dharma practitioner if your mind hasn't turned away from desire.

You may undertake various hardships, but you are not a Dharma practitioner if you cannot bear being hurt by others. You may be practicing the stages of development and completion, but you are not a Dharma practitioner if you expect to remove obstacles with divinations and shamanistic rituals. You may train in the nondual, but you are not a Dharma practitioner if you expect help from gods and fear harm from demons.

You may have entered the Mahayana path, but you are not a Dharma practitioner if you don't try to benefit sentient beings. You may act for the welfare of beings, but you are not a Dharma practitioner if your deepest aims are not embraced by bodhichitta. You may have understood the view, but you are not a Dharma practitioner if you don't heed the ripening of karma.

You may comprehend the nine gradual vehicles, but you are not a Dharma practitioner if you don't mingle your mind with the Dharma. You may practice one-pointedly all the time, but you are not a Dharma practitioner if you don't destroy the fixation on appearances as being real. You may possess the three trainings, but you are not a Dharma practitioner if you are motivated by greedy pretentiousness.

In any spiritual activity you engage, if you don't embrace it with the *threefold excellence* of preparation, main part and conclusion, you are not a Dharma practitioner. You may be spontaneous in daily activities of thought, word, and deed, but you are not a Dharma practitioner if you stray into ordinary disturbing emotions. People who cast away the practices for accomplishment right now and instead make aspirations for future accomplishment are not practitioners.

You are not a practitioner if you expect to attain fruition in the future without recognizing the natural face of your mind. You may create the karmic deeds of virtuous roots, but you are not a Dharma practitioner if you haven't parted from the eight worldly concerns.

People of the future, these eight worldly concerns are audacious demons who live in everyone, high or low. These eight are to be happy when you are praised and unhappy when blamed; happy when famous and unhappy when notorious; happy when having pleasure and unhappy when uncomfortable; and happy in gain and unhappy in loss.

You must scrutinize yourself to see whether or not all the virtuous roots you created in the past through thought, word, and deed were done with the attitudes of these eight, whether or not you possess them in your present deeds, and whether or not your planned future deeds are endowed with them. It is essential to refrain from being involved with them!

All you people of the future who are followers of Padma, no matter what Dharma practice you are engaged in, practice an unmistaken path for quickly attaining the great enlightenment of buddhahood! Practice the vast and profound meaning! Practice while possessing all the teachings of the truly and completely awakened one!

Practice while possessing the meaning of the nine gradual vehicles, in the manner of upward completeness, within the mind of a single person!27 Practice any aim or deed in the manner of recognizing that no thing whatsoever is accomplished!

Practice in the state in which all the phenomena of samsara and nirvana are the single sphere of dharmakaya! Practice exclusively in accord with these instructions of mine! Practice without doubt or hesitation concerning the fruition of enlightenment!

This was the oral advice on conduct bestowed upon the Tibetan clergy members and everyone who wishes to practice the Buddhadharma. Samaya.

May this meet with worthy people possessing the karmic connection!

The Wish-fulfilling Gem of Dedication:

⁂

Namo Ghuru Dheva Dakkini Hung

I shall now explain the *Wishfulfilling Treasury of Precious Gems*,
The method for dedicating your roots of virtue, as many as they may be,
Whatever merit you have accumulated, will accumulate, or the merit in
    which you rejoice,
Towards the great and unexcelled enlightenment.

Well now, rejoice in the resolve to dedicate these good roots made for the
benefit of a particular person toward the unexcelled state of enlightenment! For
this to happen, it is important that three factors concur: the virtuous deed to be
dedicated, the recipient, and the thought of dedication.

For a practitioner of Secret Mantra, the master is regarded as the pure field
of merit, just as the *Shri Guhyasamaja* mentions:

At the outset of any offering,
Set aside all other offerings
And commence with an offering to your master,
Since by pleasing him you attain accomplishment,
The sublime state of omniscience.

According to the sutras, it is taught the Sangha is the pure field of merit. As the *Sutra on the Furtherance of Virtue* says:

Being the treasury of all the teachings
And the opener of all doors,
The ones known as Sangha members
Are the Sangha to be supported by everyone.

In the general sense, the Three Jewels are accepted as the pure fields of merit. It is said,

There is no teacher like the Buddha.
There is no protector like the Dharma.
There is no field like the Sangha.
Thus I make this offering to the Three Jewels!

A sutra says, "The followers of the lower vehicles consider the elevated field to be supreme. For instance, when you sow seeds — the cause — in an excellent field, and carefully nurture them by supplying fertilizer, breaking up clods of dirt, and so forth, the crop — the effect — will be abundant. Likewise, the effect is magnified many times if the field of merit is pure."

The followers of Mahayana regard inferior recipients as more important and support those who are disabled, rejected, and friendless. A scripture mentions,

Those who are disheartened and friendless,
The sick and disabled,
The old, the indisposed, and those deprived of senses,
The destitute, the famished, and beggars —
Bodhisattvas should support these unprotected people.

To these pure recipients, whether high or low, the objects we offer are, in the case of the higher recipients, actually present and mentally created.

With unsurpassable offering-clouds of Samantabhadra,
Actually present and mentally created,
Vastly and fully displayed within pure space,
We present you with an ocean of outer, inner and secret offerings.28

It is taught one should give necessary articles that are uncontaminated by wrongdoing, such as wrong livelihood, to the lower recipients by means of fourfold giving, as a sutra says,

No articles from theft, robbery or monastic holdings,
Nor harmful things,
But that which is treasured and delightful,
And, at best, which is also needed.

Moreover, it is said,

Assist the poor and disabled
With the fourfold types of giving
Of provisions and a variety of pleasant sense-objects,
But not objects mixed with evil deeds or weaponry,
Nor food poisoned by improper earnings.

Motivate yourself in this way, with a pure attitude toward the pure field of merit. Generate trust in the ones above, compassion for the ones below, and the awakened mind of enlightenment. It is said,

Motivated by trust and compassion,
Give for the sake of others with the enlightened attitude.
Guide with dedication and good wishes,
And seal by not conceptualizing the three spheres.[29]

It is also said,

While possessing a pure attitude
Toward all pure objects,
Offer or give the best things.
When you dedicate them to the state of the supreme vehicle
And seal by not conceptualizing the three spheres,
This dedication is the most eminent.

In this way, the accumulation of merit is created by connecting object, article, and attitude with the virtue to be dedicated. Now, to what should these virtuous deeds be dedicated? And to which cause or end should they be dedicated?

To quote the Great Mother Prajnaparamita, "The bodhisattva spiritual guide should dedicate all virtue or good roots toward the state of complete omniscience, and not toward the state of a shravaka or pratyekabuddha."

Thus, dedicate to the cause for attaining the fruition of complete omniscience, the state of all-knowing buddhahood. Regarding the different types of masters who make the dedication, Padmavajra has said:

The ones who realize the natural state of the view,
Who are adept in the samadhi of meditation,
Who possess the compassionate enlightened mind,
And all the marks of being qualified —
Such sublime spiritual friends
Are the most eminent masters to dedicate the merit.

Best is when such a master is within reach; if not, it is said,

For whomever has supreme faith and resolve
The buddha will be present as if in person.

And also,

At the right time, such as on the new moon, full moon, and the eighth
    [of the lunar month],
Dedicate the good roots in the presence of the Three Jewels.

It is also permissible for the faithful to dedicate in the presence of a shrine for the Three Jewels.

Next, for whose sake is the dedication made? Do not dedicate just for the sake of a certain person, but for the sake of all sentient beings headed by so-and-so.30 As is said,

Directly and also indirectly,
Only do what is for the benefit of beings.
For the sake of all sentient beings,
You should dedicate all merit to their enlightenment.

For a person who is alive, simply use his or her name; for someone who has passed away, use 'the late so-and-so.'

When dedicating for the sake of all sentient beings headed by a certain person, instruct him by saying:

"Keep your body and mind respectful, join the palms, and imagine that in the sky before you sits our main teacher, the transcendent perfect conqueror, the victorious one, Buddha Shakyamuni, adorned with the numerous major and minor marks, surrounded by all the buddhas and bodhisattvas of the ten directions, as well as by the gurus, yidams, dakinis, and the loyal guardians of the Dharma. Offer your body and wealth, power and glory, and all your good roots, thinking, 'So that all sentient beings headed by so-and-so may attain supreme, true and complete enlightenment, I dedicate all the virtuous roots resulting from the merit and wisdom gathered by myself and all others since beginningless samsara!' With a respectful voice, repeat the words of the dedication."

If the dedication is made for someone else, then the word 'you' should be substituted [for 'I']. If a congregation of four [ordained sangha members] are present, request them to add their well-wishes. The master himself should personally, without wavering from the words and their meaning, focus on this resolve:

"Buddhas and bodhisattvas who dwell in the ten directions, please pay heed to so-and-so! Gurus and deities of the yidam mandala, please pay heed!

"The good roots created since beginningless samsara and resulting from giving, discipline, meditation and so forth, which the person known as so-and-so has created, caused others to create, or rejoiced in their creating, and the good roots resulting from merit and wisdom created in thought, word, and deed in this very life or in the future — just as all noble beings accomplished in the power of truth have done, I fully dedicate them as a cause for the supreme, true and complete enlightenment for the sake of so-and-so, as well as all other sentient beings!"

If the dedicator's realization is superior to your own or if he is a great master, then make the request to bear witness and change the end of the dedication and aspiration for the benefit of all sentient beings as follows:

"May all sentient beings headed by so-and-so swiftly attain the precious state of supreme, true and complete enlightenment!"

Having repeated that three times, say:

Until achieving the aim of the aspiration, throughout all lives and rebirths, may all sentient beings attain the level of a god or a human in the higher realms, without being interrupted by any other rebirth!

May they possess all the qualities of a high rebirth including the most noble character!

May they meet with a spiritual guide who upholds the lineage of sublime masters, and be accepted into his following!

Accomplished in the three pleasing ways,[31] may they enjoy the wealth of the unexcelled teachings of the supreme vehicle through learning, reflection and meditation!

Through possessing perfect dwelling place, companions, and favorable conditions, may they extensively turn the profound and serene Dharma wheel of the unexcelled and supreme vehicle!

Through immeasurable compassionate activity endowed with the boundless love and empathy of the awakened mind, may they accomplish, effortlessly and spontaneously, the welfare of all sentient beings, taming each in whatever way is appropriate!

Journeying to the all-encompassing ocean of boundless buddha realms, including the mandalas of the gurus, yidams and dakinis, may they be protected by the realization of their marvelous deeds! May they enter into the following of all these gatherings! May they follow in their footsteps! May they be equal to the buddhas in realization, compassion, deeds, and activity!

"On the path of accomplishing this, may all unwholesome and adverse elements such as difficulties, obstacles, distractions, laziness, wrongdoing, and error subside! May they possess perfect circumstances and an abundance of these qualities of well-being and happiness: long life-span, good health, attractive form, deep faith, sharp intelligence, great compassion, strong vigor, plentiful wealth, joy in giving, pure samaya commitments, perfect discipline, and so forth!

If the dedication and aspiration is made for the sake of a deceased person, at this point perform the ritual for purifying obscurations. If it is for a living person, then say any other suitable aspiration, as well as the following:

In this very life may they possess longevity, good health, and abundant wealth and excellence!

May all their sickness and evil influences, misdeeds and obscurations, transgressions, mistakes and misfortunes, their outer and inner obstacles, and all evil and discordant forces be pacified!

May they abide by the Dharma in thought, word and deed, and, while enjoying the flawless words of the victorious ones, may they have all their wishes fulfilled, just as if they possessed the wishfulfilling powerful king of precious stones!

When the time of death arrives, may they not suffer the misery of the life-force being interrupted, but may all conceptual states of disturbing emotions subside, and may they joyfully and delightfully remember their guru and the Three Jewels!

May they be completely protected by the wisdom mind of all noble beings endowed with great compassion who are the unsurpassable objects of refuge!

May they not undergo the fear and terror of the bardo, and may all the doors to the lower realms of existence be closed!

As the ultimate, may they soon attain the precious state of unexcelled, true and complete enlightenment!

By the blessings the Buddha's attainment of the three kayas,
By the blessings of the unchanging truth of dharmata,
By the blessings of the unshakable resolve of the Sangha,
And by the blessings of the guru, yidam and dakini,
May whatever I dedicate be accomplished!
May all my wishes be powerful!"

Having uttered this, conclude by sealing with the threefold purity of non-conception.

There are boundless virtues in sealing with the precious dedication in this way and making flawless aspirations. The *Sutra Requested by Unending Intelligence* mentions:

Just as a drop of water falling into the great ocean
Does not dry up until the ocean itself does,
In the same way, the virtue fully dedicated towards enlightenment
Does not vanish before enlightenment is attained.

It is also said:

In the presence of the Three Jewels,
The deity, your master, or the like,
With an attitude of faith, gather the accumulations
And thus make vast aspirations.
The virtue of this lies beyond expression!

Having gathered the accumulations of merit and wisdom, the shortcomings of failing to seal with the precious dedication are described as these four causes of depletion:

After creating a virtuous root,
To neglect dedicating, to make a perverted dedication,
To boast about it to others, or to feel regret;
These are the four causes of depletion.

Therefore, it is essential to dedicate in the following way. Imagine that an effulgence of light rays streams forth from the heart center of the Buddha and touches the body, speech and mind of the beings for whom the dedication is being made, completely purifying their misdeeds, obscurations, faults and failings. They become spheres of light which dissolve into the heart center of the Buddha. The Buddha and his retinue depart into the expanse of invisible basic space, like a rainbow vanishing into the sky. Sealing thus, by not conceptualizing the three spheres, becomes the true and supreme dedication. As Lord Maitreya said:

The extraordinary, complete dedication
That is most eminent to perform
Is the attitude free of conceptualized focus,
With the attribute of nondelusion.

He furthermore said:

Moreover, the unexcelled supreme dedication
Is to fully know that there is no real nature
In the merit created, in its fruition,
In the dedicated or in the act of dedicating.

Therefore, bury all virtue created for a particular purpose as an inexhaustible treasure mine, and complete it by sealing it with the Mahayana dedication. Then pay respect while rejoicing with heartfelt joy and gratitude.

This was the way to instruct. Samaya.

Basically speaking, when wishing to make a dedication there are three general points: the dedication that fully protects the meritorious gift of a benefactor; the dedication after an extraordinary practice of Secret Mantra or after turning the wheel of the profound Dharma; and the dedication that perfects the accumulation of merit within the basic space of original wakefulness.

The first occurs immediately after the benefactor presents the offering, or right after enjoying it. Repeat the following, or any other suitable aspiration, three times:

All buddhas and bodhisattvas dwelling in the ten directions, pay heed to this benefactor! Masters and sangha of pure monks, please pay heed!

As demonstrated by this virtuous root,
May whatever virtue the benefactor creates throughout the three times
Be dedicated to vastly increasing an inexhaustible fruition!
May unexcelled enlightenment be swiftly attained!

The second occurs at the conclusion of any outer or inner spiritual study, teaching, and meditation, or any of the [ten] spiritual activities. Dedicate in the following way:

Buddhas and bodhisattvas of the ten directions, gurus, yidams, dakinis and all mandala deities, together with your guardians and protectors, please pay heed to me!

Within the immense great mandala of Samantabhadra,
May all the virtuous roots created throughout the three times
By the guru vajra-holder and others,
And by all vajra brothers and sisters,
As exemplified by this turning of the wheel of Dharma,
Be dedicated to the attainment of perfect buddhahood!
May everyone everywhere attain the state of Samantabhadra!

Dedicate in this way and rest in the supreme true state of the ultimate.

The third occurs at the conclusion of whatever you wish to dedicate and whenever you dedicate, or at the end of any type of activity. Make this dedication from within the state of the 'great sealing':

Victorious ones and your sons of the ten directions, pay heed!
May whatever virtue created by thought, word and deed
By myself or any other of all the sentient beings
In the three times of past, present and future,
Be dedicated toward the great sphere of enlightenment!
May the supreme fruition of the unexcelled nature be attained!

At the beginning of any kind of dedication, visualize the Three Jewels before you as the witness. Imagine that they accept you with words of dedication and well-wishes. Next, utter the words of dedication while sealing without conceptualizing what you dedicate and the objects of the dedication, the deed and doer of the dedicating. At the end, remain in the state beyond word, thought and description, within which all the phenomena comprised of samsara and nirvana at first have not arisen, in between do not remain, and in the end do not cease.

Samaya.

These skillful means of bringing virtuous causes to full maturity, the oral instructions on dedication entitled *The Wishfulfilling Gem of Dedication,* were given by the vidyadhara Padmasambhava. I, Tsogyal, wrote them down in the form of notes and concealed them as a secret terma treasure. May they meet with worthy people possessing the karmic destiny!

Seal of concealment. Seal of entrustment. Seal of treasure. Samaya. Dathim.

This was revealed from the Great Cave of Puri by me, Sangye Dorje [Sangye Lingpa], a mendicant follower of Shakyamuni.

A Spur Towards
Spiritual Practice:

✧

FORMED OUT OF THE MERIT OF BEINGS in general and of the Tibetan people in particular, the magical emanation of Lord Manjushri appeared as Trisong Deutsen, the bodhisattva and king of the Dharma. With the request to construct the temple known as Samye, the Spontaneous Fulfillment of Boundless Wishes, and with the intent to spread and propagate the sacred Dharma in Tibet, he invited Lobpön Bodhisattva and took the bodhichitta vow to demonstrate the need for being motivated by the enlightened attitude of awakened mind. To demonstrate the ripening and liberation of awakened mind, he invited Padmasambhava, the great master of Uddiyana, to confer empowerments and carry *approach and accomplishment* to the limit of perfection. To demonstrate the need for spreading and causing that to flourish, he invited the pandita Vimalamitra to turn the causal and resultant wheels of the Dharma. To demonstrate the utter completeness and spontaneous perfection of the teachings of enlightened body, speech and mind, he constructed glorious Samye, the Spontaneous Fulfillment of Boundless Wishes, and held the ceremonies of consecration and investment. Thus he spread the Buddhadharma here in Tibet, and caused the teaching and practice of Sutra and Tantra to shine like the rising sun.

In particular, the great vidyadhara known under the name Padmasambhava, a miraculous emanation of the three kayas, came to Tibet through the power of his aspirations and compassion. For as long as he remained, Padmasambhava bestowed upon His Majesty the king, the other chief disciples, and all fortunate people, innumerable profound and vast instructions for ripening and liberation. Among the many instructions he gave me, Tsogyal of Kharchen, I have here written down a compilation of all the teachings on the expedient meaning as a spur towards spiritual practice. MAHAKARUNIKA SAMATI AH.

Master Padma said: Tsogyal, we must practice a teaching that brings liberation from samsara! Unless we do so, it will be extremely difficult to attain such a body with the freedoms and riches.

How difficult is it to find a human body like this? It is as difficult to find as for a pea to stick when you throw it against the temple wall, as difficult as for a tortoise sticking its head through a yoke floating on the ocean, as difficult as throwing a mustard seed through the eye of a needle standing upright.

The reason for this difficulty is that the six classes of beings are like a heap of grain. The hell beings, hungry ghosts and animals are like the bottom half, the demigods the upper half, and gods and humans are merely the tip. Compared to the other classes of beings, it seems impossible to gain a human form. Tsogyal, try to count the beings of the six realms!

Again Master Padma said: Tsogyal, if in spite of this difficulty you succeed in attaining a human body through your past merit, it is hard to practice the sacred Dharma if you fail to possess complete sense faculties and are deaf, blind or mute. If you are reborn among primitives or savages there is no opportunity to practice the sacred Dharma. If you take rebirth in a family with the nihilistic wrong views of heretical extremists, you will not enter the Buddha's teachings.

Now we have been born on the southern Jambu continent, in a civilized land where the Buddhadharma is present. We have obtained what is difficult to attain, a precious human body, and while our sense faculties are still intact, we can meet with sublime masters, have the power to choose whatever we want to do, can enter the Buddha's teachings, practice the sacred Dharma, and associate with Sangha companions. If at this time we don't apply the teachings that bring liberation and enlightenment, this precious human body will have gone to waste.

Don't return empty-handed after reaching the island of jewels; don't linger around hungry when having met the inexhaustible treasure! We must cross the ocean while we have the vessel; don't let the boat of the human body slip away!

Now is the time to separate samsara from nirvana; joyfully exert yourself in practice! Now is the dividing point between happiness and misery; don't arrange your own disaster! Now is the time when the roads leading up and down separate; don't jump into the abyss of the lower realms!

Now is the time for showing the difference between being wise or dumb; don't stupidly babble or stare! Now is the time for lasting merit; don't busy yourself and go on empty-handed! Now is the time to see who is a great or ignoble man or woman; don't seek enlightenment in profit and fame!

Now is the time to see who is a good or evil man or woman; cast away your worldly pursuits! The present moment is comparable to a single meal in one hundred days; don't act as if you had plenty of time! Now is the time when the evil of a moment's laziness will have lasting effect; joyfully exert yourself in spiritual practice! Now is the time when a single year of perseverance brings happiness for all lives to come; remain constant in Dharma practice!

I have constant pity for the beings who leave this life empty-handed!

Again Master Padma said: Tsogyal, we don't know whether this human body, obtained with such great difficulty, will die tomorrow or the day after, so don't make plans to live forever! We cannot be certain when this body, on loan from the four elements, will fall apart, so don't treasure it too fondly!

Birth leads to nothing other than death; train in the nature of nonarising as your destination! Meeting leads to nothing other than parting; cut your attachment to companionship! Gathering leads to nothing other than depletion; be generous without clinging! Building leads to nothing other than destruction; keep to caves and mountain retreats!

Desire and ambition lead to nothing other than pain; loosen your craving! Deluded experience leads to nothing other than delusion; destroy dualistic perception! By doing so you will always be happy — but who listens to beneficial advice!

Again Master Padma said: Tsogyal, I have told this to everyone, but nobody listens. As soon as the Mara of Death catches hold of you, there is no chance for liberation. Those who do not practice the Dharma will regret this when approaching death.

The years, months and days pass by without lingering even a second. This life runs out without pausing for even an hour or a minute, and then we die. The seasons continue, but your life finishes and doesn't wait.

Don't you despair, seeing that death draws closer while the years, months and days go by? How can you feel content when everyone dies unexpectedly and suddenly? How can you be content with your offspring and wealth when they are of no use at the time of death? How can you feel so confident, when accompanied by nothing but good and evil deeds?

Those who don't cut their attachment to concrete reality and the view of permanence have no sense!

Again Master Padma said: Tsogyal, there is no way to attain a human body while in the unfree states, so it's needless to mention practicing the Dharma and attaining liberation![32]

Right now we have the power to choose whatever we want to do, yet people claim to be unable to apply the Dharma. Having obtained a human body with the freedoms and riches, they claim to not have time for spiritual practice. Fully able to constantly slave for food and clothing, they claim to be unable to practice the sacred Dharma for even a year. Tireless in samsaric bustle, they claim to be unable to bear even the smallest hardship in what concerns the Dharma. While able to undergo painful experiences unceasingly, they claim to be unable to spend even a summer or winter in the happiness of spiritual practice.

People heedless of the Dharma seem not to want happiness!

Again Master Padma said: Tsogyal, it is of utmost importance to exert yourself in spiritual practice while you are young. Once you grow old you may want to listen to teachings but your ears won't hear. You may wish to study but your attention is dull and your memory fails. You may want to go to the Dharma, but your body is unable to walk or sit. You may wish to practice, but the strength of the elements has waned and you cannot concentrate. You may want to give away your material possessions but they are controlled by others and you are not in charge. You may want to undertake hardship but your constitution cannot bear strain. Having displeased your master and Dharma companions, when old age arrives, you may want to practice but cannot. You will wish, 'If I had just had the will when I was young,' but that doesn't help. It is too late to regret not doing any spiritual practice when you were able.

People who don't feel any interest in Dharma practice when young are no better than fools!

Again Master Padma said: Tsogyal, when practicing the Dharma of liberation, to be married and lead a family life is like being restrained in tight chains with no freedom. You may wish to flee, but you have been caught in the dungeon of samsara with no escape. You may later regret it, but you have sunk into the mire of emotions, with no getting out. If you have children, they may be lovely but they are the stake that ties you to samsara. If you don't have children, the worry that your family dies out is even greater. If you have material things, between raising cattle and farming, there is no leisure to practice the Dharma. If you don't, the pain and struggle of not having food is even greater. If you have servants and workers, you are utterly carried away by being a slave to management. If you don't, your lack of power makes you controlled by others, with no freedom to practice the Dharma. In this way both the present life and your future is destroyed.

In any case, people who marry and become householders submerge themselves in the swamp of misery with no chance for liberation!

Again Master Padma said: Tsogyal, the joys of this world are extremely fickle, but if you can practice the sacred Dharma your happiness will last long. The wealth of this world is transient and passing, but if you can continuously gather the accumulations, you are truly rich. People who involve themselves in evil deeds have no sense, but those who do what is good are sensible and wise. The people who commit themselves to meaningful teachings are honorable, but those who pursue pointless gain and fame are reckless and immoral. Worldly fame and material gain are the houselords of misery; noble is the one who attains buddhahood in a single life.

People who cling to this world never find the chance to be free from samsara!

Again Master Padma said: Tsogyal, disturbing emotions arise due to circumstances, so flee the land of love and hatred. Obstacles are invoked by being distracted, so keep to a sublime master as to medicine. Poverty and sorrow in this life result from former actions, so live in unpeopled hermitages. Wrongdoing is created due to circumstances, so avoid bad company as you would poison. Pitfalls are brought about by wrong views, so study and reflect open-mindedly. Ups and downs befall everyone, both the living and the dead, so don't put the blame on others. Whatever joy and happiness befalls you, it results from your own merit, so don't be proud. Try to attain enlightenment while you have the power to avoid going into the lower realms of samsara.

People who live in evil deeds will suffer for a long while!

Again Master Padma said: Tsogyal, broadly speaking, your death has no fixed time; it has accompanied you since the day you were born. The circumstance by which you will die is also uncertain; you still die even when not intending to. Your death will never forsake you, and you may amass all the world's riches but still must leave them behind.

Samsara doesn't disappear once you die; again you will roam through the three realms. There is no happiness in samsaric existence; you never transcend misery no matter where you are reborn among the six classes of beings. How much have you roamed about in the past, undergoing untold pain! And you will continue to roam through samsara, tossed about on the waves of suffering. Wouldn't it be better to practice the Dharma and cut your chains to misery! Unless you reach dry land yourself you cannot lead others out of samsara. But it seems all Dharma practitioners cling to worldly entertainments and repeatedly throw themselves back into samsara.

With the help of the freedoms and riches, you must cut the ties to samsara right now!

Again Master Padma said: Tsogyal, unless you attain liberation now, you will only sink further in the misery of existence, regardless of where your next rebirth is. Unless you live in mountain hermitages you only live in the prison of samsara, no matter where you dwell. Unless you engage in spiritual practice you only create evil karma for further samsara, no matter what you do.

Unless you gather the two accumulations, anything else you gather only becomes the treachery of Mara. Unless you follow a spiritual teacher, anyone else you follow is only a guide into further samsara. Unless you listen to the oral instructions of your master, anyone else you listen to is only an advisor to pull you further down.

Unless the spiritual qualities take birth within your stream of being, any company is only a support for wrongdoing. Unless you realize the innate nature of your mind, any thought, no matter what, is only conceptual thinking. Unless you can steer you own mind, whatever you do only perpetuates delusion. Unless you weary of samsara, whatever you do is only seeds for the lower realms.

People who aren't disenchanted with samsara will suffer incessantly!

Again Master Padma said: Tsogyal, nothing else will help you when facing death, so do like this! Find a master who embodies the teachings of Mahayana. Receive the oral instructions that embody the true realization of the nature of mind.

Seek and keep to a safe retreat place where necessities are available. Practice with unceasing diligence. Fill your treasury without lazily procrastinating.[33]

Keep companions who are devoted, persevering, and intelligent. Practice teachings that lead you on the path of liberation. Shun like poison evil deeds that lead to the lower realms. Remain saturated by compassion, the root of the Mahayana. As your primary purpose, train in emptiness free of concepts.

Unless you give up distractions it will be hard to accomplish anything through spiritual practice!

Again Master Padma said: Tsogyal, haven't you heard that your forefathers and ancestors died? Haven't you seen that your peers and neighbors die? Haven't you noticed that your relatives die, whether they be old or young? Haven't you ever seen a corpse being carried off to the cemetery? How is it possible that you don't remember that death will come to you, too? If you remain unmotivated, the time to attain liberation will never arrive!

The very root of virtuous qualities is to take impermanence to heart, so never ever forget the fear of death! Among all notions, impermanence is the most eminent, so never be apart from it! The attitude of believing that things last is the very root of all wrongdoing, so pull it up! Unless you take this attitude [of impermanence] sincerely to heart, evil will heap up like a mountain.

To make this clear: ordinary people do not seek liberation; the dignitary is conceited and clings to his inflated self-esteem; the rich are shackled by avarice; the ignorant bask in evil deeds; the lazy live in apathy; the practitioner reverts to worldliness; the Dharma teacher strays into the eight worldly concerns; and the meditator, lacking devotion and diligence, pursues the aims of this life. All this is due to failing to take impermanence to heart.

Once the thought of impermanence is genuinely assimilated in your stream of being, all the qualities of the path of liberation will heap up like a mountain. So form the attitude of having no task whatsoever to carry out! Form the attitude that mundane aims are futile! Cast away the pointlessness of this world!

Embark on the path of liberation with fortitude! Don't cling to material things! Don't fixate on the five aggregates as being yourself! Understand that diversions are Mara! Understand that desirable sense objects are trickery! Never be apart from a sense of urgency!

Regard the affairs of this life as your enemy! Seek a true master! Flee from evil companionship! Flee to the solitude of mountain dwellings! Don't delay your spiritual practice! Observe your vows and samayas! Mingle your mind with the Dharma!

If you do like this, the yidam will bestow the siddhis, the dakinis will grant their blessings, the buddhas will give you assurance, and you will soon reach enlightenment — all this results from taking impermanence to heart.

From the past and till this very day, all the buddhas and their sons and daughters, and all the vidyadharas and siddhas were liberated from samsara by taking this to heart!

Again Master Padma said: Tsogyal, you fall into the lower realms through the ten nonvirtues, so repent and vow to refrain from even the smallest evil! Virtue with a conceptual focus does not become the path of liberation, so embrace any spiritual practice you do with the nonconceptual state! Virtuous actions created over aeons can still be destroyed by a single moment of hatred, so train in love, compassion, and the enlightened frame of mind! You may have understood emptiness, but it turns into nihilism unless you can be compassionate, so equalize compassion and emptiness!

In any case, nothing is of any avail unless you abandon the clinging to things as being concrete, so don't regard your deluded experience to be solid reality!

Again Master Padma said: Tsogyal, unless you immediately cast samsaric existence behind you, your karma and disturbing emotions, as the cause, will surely make you take rebirth in a conditioned body, as the result. As soon as you take such a rebirth, that body is of a painful nature. After taking birth, aging and death inevitably follow. And as soon as death happens there is definitely no other destination than rebirth among the six classes of beings.

Reborn in such a form, desire and misery automatically exist; there is no escaping the painful ocean of karmic deeds created through the five poisons. The logical conclusion of failing to escape is that you spin incessantly in samsaric existence. To escape that you must realize the nonarising of your mind. Unless you realize that, there is no liberation from samsara!

Again Master Padma said: Tsogyal, samsara in general has neither beginning nor end, but you as an individual must experience its beginning and end! You may be powerful and rich during this life, but it is of no avail since you must still depart. Your strength, power and abilities may be great, but that won't overcome the Mara of Death.

You may have wealth and luxuries but that won't fool the Lord of Death once you're in his grasp. Your legions and wealth may be formidable, but they will neither ride ahead nor follow behind. Your offspring, attendants, and relatives may be numerous, but they cannot accompany you into the next life. You may surround yourself with all the armies in the world, but they cannot hold back the onslaught of birth, old age, sickness and death.

Unless you guarantee now the welfare of your future lives, who can bear the pain of falling into the hells? The hunger and thirst of the hungry ghosts are intolerable! The enslavement of animals is dreadful! The changes of human life are mostly painful! The strife of the demigods is unendurable! The fall of the gods is excruciating! All beings spin around in this vicious circle. The waves of birth and death are hard to escape!

All is pointless unless you cross the abyss of the six classes of beings. To cross that you must develop the strength of nondual awareness!

Again Master Padma said: Tsogyal, if you wish to be free of samsaric existence, then do like this.

Your ordinary attachment and aversion are mistaken, deluded thinking: cut it in itself! The belief in a self is the root and basis of samsara: uproot it! Companions and relatives are the chain that pulls you down: sever your ties! The thought of enemies and demons is a torture for your mind: cast it away!

Indifference cuts the life-force of liberation: leave it behind! Fraud and deceit are a heavy load: cast it away! Envy is the hailstorm that destroys all goodness: eliminate your own faults! Your homeland is a demonic prison: avoid it like a poison!

Desirable sense objects are the ties that confine you: cut your bondage! Harsh words are a poisonous weapon: hold your tongue! Ignorance is the darkest defilement: light the lamp of study and reflection! Lovers, spouse and offspring are the ruse of Mara: curtail your attachment! Whatever you experience is delusion: let it be freed in itself!

If you do like this, you will turn away from samsaric existence!

Again Master Padma said: Tsogyal, when you understand the faults of samsara, there is no teacher to seek apart from that. When you have taken impermanence to heart, there is no encouragement to depend upon apart from that. When you realize all that appears and exists to be your mind, there is no path of enlightenment apart from that.

When you have firm devotion to your master, there is no buddha to find apart from that. When you delight all sentient beings, there are no Three Jewels to worship apart from that. When you cut the basis and root of thought, there is no innate nature to meditate upon apart from that. When samsaric existence is freed in itself, there is no awakened state to accomplish apart from that. Once you realize this, samsara and nirvana are not two.

Otherwise, youth is brief while troubles are many. Forgetfulness is strong while the remedies are weak. Inspiration is feeble while distractions are numerous. Diligence is scarce while laziness abounds. Mundane tasks are innumerable while dharmic deeds are few. Evil thoughts are foremost while intelligence is minimal.

Oh, how much the people of the dark age will regret at the verge of death! Tsogyal, you must receive the profound oral instructions!

Again Master Padma said: Tsogyal, to escape samsaric existence you must have faith in the path of liberation. That is to say, faith arises through causes and conditions and not on its own. Faith arises when causes and conditions coincide and you take impermanence to heart. Faith arises when remembering cause and effect.

Faith arises when reading the profound sutras and tantras. Faith arises when associating with faithful companions. Faith arises when following a master and spiritual teacher. Faith arises when being in painful difficulties.

Faith arises when making offerings at a special shrine. Faith arises when encountering profound behavior. Faith arises when hearing the life examples of the lineage masters. Faith arises when listening to the vajra songs of realization.

Faith arises when seeing the suffering of another being. Faith arises when contemplating the defects of samsaric existence. Faith arises when reading the sacred teachings of your inclination. Faith arises when noticing the qualities of sublime beings. Faith arises when receiving the blessings of your master. Faith arises when gathering the special accumulations.

It is my advice to never be apart from the causes for faith to arise.

Again Master Padma said: Tsogyal, if you have faith in your heart you must make it endure. If you don't, you must make it arise!

To lack faith is like trying to make charcoal white: you are severed from the virtues of the path of liberation. To lack faith is like being a gemstone at the bottom of the ocean: you are enmeshed in the depths of samsaric existence. To lack faith is like being in a boat without oars: you cannot cross the sea. To lack faith is like sowing grains in rigid and uncultivated though fertile soil: not a single virtue survives.

To lack faith is like a seed that has been scorched by fire: the sprouts of enlightenment don't grow. To lack faith is like traveling through fearful places without an escort: you won't overcome the enemy of disturbing emotions. To lack faith is like being a vagrant landing in jail: you won't escape the lower realms. To lack faith is like an armless man trying to climb a rock: you fall into the abyss of the six classes of beings.

To lack faith is like a deer caught by the hunter: you will be executed by the Lord of Death. To lack faith is like a blind man staring at a shrine: you don't see the object of knowledge. To lack faith is like an idiot arriving on an island of pure gold: you don't know what you have found.

People without faith cannot possibly attain liberation or enlightenment!

Again Master Padma said: Tsogyal, for attaining enlightenment, to have faith is to complete half the practice of the Dharma.

Faith is like a fertile field: any instruction planted will grow. Faith is like a wishfulfilling jewel: it yields the blessings to accomplish whatever one pursues. Faith is like a world ruler: it upholds the kingdom of the Dharma. Faith is like a strong castle: it withstands the disturbing emotions of self and others.

Faith is like a bridge or a boat: it allows you to cross the ocean of samsara. Faith is like a rope dangling into an abyss: it pulls you out of the lower realms. Faith is like a healing physician: it eliminates the chronic disease of the five poisons. Faith is like a powerful escort: it leads you safely through the perils of samsara.

Faith is like a protective defender: it saves you from the treacherous four Maras. Faith is like the waxing moon: it lets virtues increase further and further. Faith is like a bribe to dodge imprisonment: it tricks the demonic Lord of Death. Faith is like an ascending pathway: it leads you to the elevated city.

Faith is like an inexhaustible treasure mine: it provides for all needs and wants. Faith is like a man's hands: it gathers the roots of virtue. Faith is like a swift-footed steed: it carries you to the point of liberation. Faith is like an elephant who can carry a huge load: it leads you higher and higher. Faith is like a sparkling fountainhead: it manifests innate wakefulness.

Once faith has dawned from deep within you, all virtuous qualities arrive in a mountainous heap!

Again Master Padma said: Tsogyal, the root of all the virtues of buddhahood rests on faith, so let an unchanging faith arise from deep within you! It prevents the unfree states and earns the freedoms and riches. It detaches you from evil companions and makes you follow a genuine master. It closes the door to the lower realms and shows the start of the path of liberation.

It dispels doubt and hesitation and leads you beyond the ways of Mara. It inhibits conceit and envy and causes you to achieve the freedoms and riches. It frees you from the defects of evil deeds and lets you attain everything wholesome. It makes you transcend objects of attachment and gain trust in total surrender.

It lets you abandon wrong views and behavior and gain trust in the teachings of the victorious ones. It utterly dispels disturbing emotions and lets you discover self-existing virtues. It makes you cross the ocean of existence and become a true guide. It decreases nonvirtue and increases all that is virtuous. It discards mistaken counsel and makes you accomplish the ultimate essence.

Compared to serving sentient beings in a number equal to the dust motes in ten buddha realms, the tantras teach that faith in the Mahayana teachings is of greater merit!

Again Master Padma said: Tsogyal, if people will listen, this is the instruction they should practice!

Enough with your past struggling with pointless activities: now accomplish the important task! Enough with your tiresome and hopeless slaving for others: now accomplish the necessary benefit for yourself! Enough with your wasted words and deeds enacted due to the five poisons: now steer you body and voice to the Dharma! Enough with your unconcerned complacency: now bring forth joyous diligence in practice!

Enough with your submitting to relatives: break down the wall of fearfulness! Enough with hatred towards enemies and demons: now train in love and compassion! Enough with being caught up in the six sense objects: now look into the natural state of mind![34] Enough with your creation of evil karma: now give up misdeeds and wrongdoing!

Enough with your misery in samsaric existence: now escape to the realm of great bliss! Enough with your gathering in groups of many: now live in solitude! Enough with your unwholesome words: now be silent and keep company with the truth! Enough with your deluded thinking and planning: now recognize dharmakaya, your natural face!

Now is the time for unifying faith and diligence and for accomplishing the awakened state!

Again Master Padma said: Tsogyal, until attaining enlightenment you need a master, so keep company with an authentic spiritual teacher. Until realizing the natural state you need to learn, so receive the profound oral instructions. You don't awaken to enlightenment by mere intellectual comprehension, so be diligent in practice, like lighting a fire. Until you reach stability in the innate nature you are still prone to obstacles, so give up distracting business. Until you reach the final destination you need to foster good qualities, so train gradually in strengthening awareness.

Keep distant from whatever harms your thought, word, and deed, and always remain relaxed. Avoid company that promotes disturbing emotions and focus on friends who encourage you to virtue. At morning, night and in the breaks count up your virtuous and evil deeds and place your mind on guard. You may possess the oral instructions but their purpose is wasted unless you put them into training, so practice whatever you have understood.

Results follow automatically from carrying out whatever your master instructs, so listen to the sacred Dharma!

Again Master Padma said: Tsogyal, food and clothing will appear automatically when you sincerely practice the Dharma.

Like drinking salt water, desires are unquenchable, so remain content! Eliminate your inflated self-esteem and remain gentle and disciplined! Honor and respect are the snares of Mara, so throw them out like stones on a river's bank! Pleasure and good reputation are only fleeting, so leave the affairs of this life behind with total disregard. Future lives lasts longer than the present life, so furnish yourself with the most eminent provisions!

We must leave this life alone and friendless, so seek the escort of fearlessness! Do not scorn the meek; make no distinction between high and low! Do not envy the qualified; adopt their qualities yourself! Do not ponder the flaws of others; remove your own faults as carefully as hairs on your face! Do not be concerned for your own well-being; worry about the happiness of others and be kind to all.

Arouse the four immeasurables and foster all beings like your children! Weigh the sutras and tantras as carefully as wool, and assimilate the scriptures within your stream of being! Churn through the kingdoms like you would buttermilk, and seek the most profound instructions! Everything is experienced through former karma and not through craving, so rest your mind at ease!

To be scorned by sublime masters is worse than death, so be honest and free from deceit! The troubles of this life are due to former karma, so don't put the blame on others! Well-being is the blessings of your master, so take care to repay his kindness! Without taming yourself you cannot influence others, so tame yourself first! Without higher perceptions you cannot accomplish the welfare of beings, so be diligent in practice!

Again Master Padma said: Tsogyal, if people care for themselves, they should listen to my instructions!

We must leave behind all accumulated riches, so don't do evil for the sake of wealth! The karmic ripening of good and evil deeds does not disappear for aeons, so take care with even the subtlest form of cause and effect! Transient possessions have no substance, so use them for meritorious acts of giving! The virtue created in the present you will need in the future, so observe pure discipline!

Hatred is rampant during the dark age, so wear the armor of patience! Through laziness you will again go astray into samsaric existence, so generate undistracted diligence! Your life runs out on the road of distraction, so train in meditation and the innate nature! Ignorance torments you in samsaric existence, so kindle the lamp of knowledge!

There is no happiness in this swamp of filth, so proceed to the dry land of liberation! Train correctly in the profound instructions and cut through the web of existence! Forsake your homeland, keep distant from relatives, and live in mountain retreats! Give up diversions in thought, word, and deed, and look into your unconfined innate nature!

Take the lowest seat, wear ragged clothes, and maintain your experience! Eat simple food, meander like the rivers in India, and unearth the heart-treasury of sublime beings! You won't find flawless sentient beings, so don't dwell on the faults of your master and Dharma friends!

This life is all superficial reality: don't wallow in hope and fear, but train in everything being an illusion! In order to benefit beings in the future you must cultivate the bodhisattva resolve! The two obscurations hinder the arising of good qualities, so purify them quickly!

If you fear this state of samsara which is like a mansion in flames, you should heed these instructions of Padma!

Again Master Padma said: Tsogyal, if you wish to be constant in your practice, then cut your attachments directly!

When the forbidding armies of super-knowledges arrive, surround yourself with the iron wall of seeing them as illusion![35] When you get angry at an unfriendly word, seek the source of that echo! To develop the wakefulness of vipashyana, use sights and sounds as methods! If you wish to perfect the strength of experience, develop your skill through enhancement practices!

To pass through the stages of the path of noble beings, look into the view of means and knowledge! If you wish to have inexhaustible wealth, then gather the property of the two accumulations! If you wish to cross the perilous places of wrong views, then free your mind of the confines of dualistic perception! If you wish the wisdom of great bliss to grow within your stream of being, then receive the direct instructions on the path of means!

If you wish to be always happy, then escape this prison of misery! If you wish to realize the rootless essence of mind, then cut your attachment to meditation experience! If you wish to be soaked in the steady rain of blessings, then supplicate with devotion! If you wish to cross over the abyss of the six classes of beings, then exorcise the evil spirit of ego! If you wish to fulfill the noble aspiration of the Buddhadharma, then sever your ties to your present experience!

If you wish to train in the wakefulness of vipashyana, then don't leave nondual awareness on the threshold of indecision! If you wish to mingle your heart with the Dharma, then don't let your practice turn numb and insensitive! If you wish to complete your task within this very lifetime, don't leave the stage of fruition as a mere aspiration! If you wish to experience what appears and exists as original wakefulness, then look into the natural state of your mind!

Tsogyal, there don't seem to be any practitioners who practice correctly!

Again Master Padma said: Tsogyal, to benefit future generations, give precepts that fit their capacity; give instructions that fit their level of intelligence; give practices that fit their degree of diligence!

Understand that and teach whatever you personally have trust in. Otherwise, the intelligent person instructed in what is not interesting will remain unsatisfied, which will diminish his faith and cause the misdeed of making someone lose faith.

The person of lesser intelligence instructed in the higher definitive meaning will not comprehend it. Even though understanding, some may feel frightened and malign the teachings. Some will grasp onto words which they don't understand and reap more harm than benefit.[36]

As the wise masters advise, an ordinary disciple of lesser intelligence instructed in the ultimate and unexcelled teachings will not connect with the true Dharma, but, feeling confident at have grasped mere words, will regress and fail to understand.

To teach that there is no need to study and reflect diminishes the already low level of knowledge and increases the already present ignorance. To teach that the Dharma involves nothing to do decreases already weak diligence and adds to already present laziness. To teach that there is no cause and effect lessens the already small amount of virtue and bolsters the already present superficial understanding.

To teach that there is no good and evil cripples whatever little devotion one has and swells the conceit already present. To teach that there is no birth and death undermines already weak faith and enhances the already large amount of wrong views. To teach that there is no samsara and nirvana depletes one's already feeble interest in attaining fruition and fortifies the already powerful eight worldly concerns.

This creates more wrong views than benefit!

Again Master Padma said: Tsogyal, unless you weary of suffering you won't renounce worldly affairs, even though you contemplate the faults of samsaric existence. Unless impermanence sincerely takes root in your mind you won't cut your attachment to appearances, even though you see the changes of conditioned things. Unless you keep company with the uncertainty of the time of death you can't take the profound instructions to heart, even though you been taught them.

Unless you resolve the unreality of deluded experience, you won't surrender clinging to a concrete reality, even though you understand it to be a lure of magical illusion. Unless you abandon worldly affairs you can't separate samsara and nirvana, even though your vessel is full of profound instructions. Unless you seize the royal stronghold right now, it's not clear where your negative karma will take you, even though you may have generated some positive karma for the future.

Unless you sincerely turn away from striving after samsara, you won't reach the end of meditation practice, though you may feel faith once or twice. Unless you forsake family life and attachment to your homeland, you won't rise above the swamp of samsaric existence, even though you exert yourself resolutely. Unless you untangle yourself from the objects of ego-clinging, you won't block the river leading into the six classes of beings, even though you understand that the three realms have no real substance.

Unless you mingle your mind with the path of liberation, you won't be able to bless the experience of others, though you may be learned in the five topics of knowledge. Unless you eradicate you own inner faults the vile zombie of disturbing emotions will rise again, even though you have glimpsed the blissful and clear state of wakefulness. Unless you cut the bond of longing, you will return again and again, even though you have relinquished the objects of like and dislike.

If your secular affairs are too numerous you will not find the chance to attain the awakened state, even though you have obtained the oral instructions of a master. You may study and reflect constantly, but unless fear of birth and death strikes your heart all the teachings will be no more than words. You may attain proficiency in the four activities, but unless you work for the welfare of beings your bodhisattva resolve will be superfluous.

Your armor of discipline may be impressive, but unless you attain the acceptance of the innate nature, it won't withstand harsh words. You may be learned in the outer and inner teachings, but unless you exert yourself in practice, your mind won't rise above that of a commoner. Your master may have virtues as great as a gathering of cloud banks, but unless you, the disciple, possess the field of devotion, the rain of blessings won't fall.

As a practitioner you may have received the blessings and oral instructions, but unless you have immeasurable compassion, it won't benefit sentient beings. You may obtain a castle in the world of man, but unless you seize the royal stronghold of nonarising, you will roam about chaotically in the afterlife. Unless you keep the companion of unfailing realization, your friends and relatives may be many, but you will still die, leaving them all behind.

You may have achieved all the martial arts of bravery, but unless you perfect the strength of meditation while in this body, you won't resist the armies of the Lord of Death. Your eloquence may be heart-rending, but unless you resolve wholeheartedly to attain liberation, it won't move the Lord of Death. Unless you cultivate the field of lasting value right now, you can spend your entire life accumulating wealth, but there will come a time when you can't bring along a single grain of wheat.

Many conducive circumstances must coincide in order to attain buddha-hood in a single life, and that is difficult!

Again Master Padma said: Tsogyal, it seems that most Tibetan Dharma practitioners have surely not taken the teachings to heart! If they had, they couldn't possibly be so lazy and unconcerned. They surely haven't understood the nature of samsara; if they had, they couldn't possibly be so attached to a solid reality. They surely never contemplate these hard-to-find freedoms and riches; if they did, they wouldn't be involved in such pointless activities.

They surely don't understand the law of cause and effect; if they did, they would be extremely careful to avoid evil deeds. They can't possibly see the good qualities of virtuous deeds; if they did, they would be tireless in gathering the two accumulations. They must not have any experience of the profound innate nature; if they did, they wouldn't dare to separate themselves from practice.

They can't possibly have come close to forming the Mahayana resolve; if they had, they would totally disregard selfish aims and work for the welfare of others.[37] They must not have directed their minds towards the innate nature; if they had, they would surely be free from envy and conceit. They can't possibly have studied or reflected upon the nine gradual vehicles; if they had, they would understand the difference between the higher and lower teachings.

Surely they haven't approached the view of Secret Mantra; if they had, they would know what to accept and reject concerning samsara and nirvana. They must not have realized the true view of the natural state; if they had, they would surely not behave in such base and prejudiced ways. They can't possibly have any wish to awaken to perfect enlightenment; if they had, they would spurn the futile affairs of this life.

There are many people without even the slightest interest in the Dharma!

Again Master Padma said: Tsogyal, I have the instruction if you wish to mingle your mind with the Dharma.

The sutras and tantras are unfailing witnesses, so conform with the teachings in whatever you do. The master's advice is the final counsel, so follow the words of sublime beings. Your yidam is the support for accomplishment, so practice unwaveringly. Your obstacles are removed by the guardians, so rely on the dakinis and *Dharma protectors.*

Your task is to engage in spiritual practices, so never be apart from Dharma practice in thought, word, and deed. What you experience is deluded perception, so consider whatever appears as being unreal. What you should tame is ego-clinging, so expel the evil spirit of selfishness. What you should give is well-being to others, so protect sentient beings as you would your own child.

What you should realize is the view, so recognize that samsara and nirvana are the innate nature. What you should dispel are obstacles, so perceive adversity as a helper. What you should attain is buddhahood, so realize the three kayas. Your mind is mingled with the Dharma when you possess all these, but most people don't complete the path of liberation.

Again Master Padma said: Tsogyal, when the end of the age [of the Buddhadharma] draws near, there will be many people here in Tibet who wish to reach enlightenment, but as they will need to know how to practice the Dharma correctly, only a few will succeed. If at that time they will listen to this kind advice, they have a way to attain happiness.

I beg you to give us that advice, she said.

The master replied: You may exert yourself painstakingly, but you won't escape the demon of obstacles as long as you live in the city, so if you wish to quickly attain accomplishment, live in secluded mountain dwellings. You may have formed the Mahayana resolve, but it is strenuous to work for the welfare of others without having reached maturity yourself, so bring the practice into personal experience. You may possess the view of the definitive meaning, but unless you are skilled during daily activities you slip into the five poisons of an ordinary person, so renounce mundane affairs.

You may pursue spiritual practices that appear to be Dharma, but if you lose the bodhisattva resolve you drift into the ways of a worldly person, so give up the eight worldly concerns. You may have been accepted with the master's compassion, but unless you cast away worldly concerns you won't cut the bonds of friend and enemy, so give up clinging to the duality of self and other. You may have received the profound instructions, but that alone won't eliminate obstacles if you do not persevere, so utilize skillful means for progress.

You may be concentrated during the meditation state, but unless you manage to include adversity on the path it won't cut the powerful flow of habitual tendencies, so experience your innate nature during the ensuing knowledge [of the post-meditation state]. Your spiritual practice with concepts may be unceasing, but it will turn into hope and fear concerning fruition unless you can release your ambition into the nonconceptual state, so untie the knot of dualistic fixation.

Your knowledge of the sutras and tantras may be extensive, but unless you realize the natural state of mind you will remain a commoner when your mind leaves the body, so recognize the true nature of practice. You may aim at accomplishment, but unless you remain a worthy vessel for the samayas you will demonstrate a preference for a particular yidam, so keep your samayas pure.

In any case, those people who enter the Buddhadharma but don't act in accordance with the sutras and tantras and the word of their master will not find happiness! But if they listen to the advice of the Lotus-Born master of Uddiyana, they will be happy in this life and joyous in the following.

Again Master Padma said: Tsogyal, during the dreadful winter of the final age people will suffer like this: the king's law will decline like the setting sun, and the religious principles of his subjects will break like a silken knot. The study and teaching of the Dharma all over the world will vanish like snowflakes falling on water; those who reflect and meditate will be scarcer than stars at dawn; qualified masters who aim to benefit others will disappear like a stone thrown into a well; and all the different species of animals will be cut down like crops at harvest and be nothing more than tales from past generations. Spiritual teachers who are like boats and bridges will vanish in the water of great bondage; people with good qualities will disappear like grass and bushes swept away by the cosmic wind, and the teachings of Buddha Shakyamuni will fade like shadows at dusk.

When that age arrives, your kindly spoken words will be heard as rebuke and diatribe. When telling others to practice the Dharma, they will reply 'Do it yourself!' When teaching about the buddha mind they will feign comprehension while missing the point. When teaching trust in the law of karma, they will say, 'It's not true, it is false!'

At that time people will kill as their way of life; as trade they will deal in falsehood; wearing costumes to bolster their confidence, they will murder for prizes and revel in sexual perversity. Making goods and possessions their main aim, they will slaughter living beings as a religious act and feast on them. Such are the times that will come.

At that time, those who practice my advice will benefit both themselves and other destined people of future generations. Therefore, Tsogyal of Kharchen, for the sake of people in the future commit this to writing and conceal it as a terma treasure.

Thus Padmasambhava spoke.

THE ASPIRATION OF THE VAJRADHATU MANDALA:

❧

NAMO GURU. On the tenth day of the monkey month in the monkey year, the Master of Uddiyana uttered this aspiration on the occasion of revealing the vajradhatu mandala in the turquoise-covered middle chamber of Samye. Thereafter, the king and the disciples made it their daily practice. All future generations should wholeheartedly adopt it as their practice as well.

Victorious ones and your sons in the ten directions and four times,
Assemblies of gurus, yidams, dakinis, and dharma protectors
Please come here all of you, numerous as dust motes in the world
And be seated on the lotus and moon seats in the sky before me.

With respectful body, speech, and mind I bow down
And present to you outer, inner, secret, and suchness offerings.
In the presence of you sugatas, the supreme objects of worship,
I feel shame for my past evil actions
And regretfully confess my present nonvirtues.
I shall restrain myself and turn away from them in the future.

I rejoice in all the gatherings of merit and virtue
And ask you, victorious ones, not to pass away into nirvana
But to turn the Dharma wheel of the Tripitaka and the unexcelled
    teachings.
All accumulations of virtue I dedicate to the minds of beings,
So they may reach unsurpassable liberation.

Buddhas and your sons, please listen to me!
May this excellent aspiration which I have here begun
Be expressed in accordance with
The victorious Samantabhadra and his sons
And with the wisdom of noble Manjushri.

May all the precious masters, the splendor of the doctrine,
Reach everywhere like the sky.
May they shine on everyone like the sun and moon
And may their lives be firm as mountains.

May the precious sangha, the foundation of the doctrine,
Be in harmony, keep pure vows and be wealthy in the three trainings.
May the practitioners of Mantrayana, the essence of the doctrine,
Keep their samaya and perfect the development and completion stages.

May the ruler who supports the Dharma, the patron of the doctrine,
Expand his dominion and aid the Buddhist teachings.
May the nobility and chieftains, the servants of the doctrine,
Increase their intelligence and be endowed with resourcefulness.

May all rich householders, the sponsors of the doctrine,
Have wealth and enjoyment and be free from harm.
May all the countries with faith in the doctrine
Have peace and happiness and be free from obstacles.

May I, a yogi on the path,
Have flawless samaya and fulfillment of my wishes.
May anyone connected with me through good or evil karma,
Both now and ultimately, be cherished by the victorious ones.
May all beings enter the gate of the unexcelled vehicle
And attain the vast kingdom of Samantabhadra.

Exert yourself in this aspiration during the six sessions.
Samaya, seal.

The great treasure revealer Chokgyur Lingpa, emanation of Prince Murub, revealed this treasure among a crowd of people. He took it from underneath the upper part of Piled Jewels Rock Mountain, situated on the right slope of the most sacred place, Sengchen Namtrak. The silk paper, made from the robe of Vairochana with Tibetan *shurma* letters written by Tsogyal, was then immediately and accurately transcribed by Padma Garwang Lodrö Thaye. May virtuous goodness increase.

NOTES

1. The literal meaning of the Tibetan word *gom,* to 'meditate,' is to 'cultivate,' in the sense of bringing forth something which is not already there. The training of the Great Perfection is not an 'act of meditating' in the sense of creating and keeping something in mind. *Tulku Urgyen Rinpoche*

2. The other source says 'distraction' rather than 'conviction.'

3. The Lama Gongdü version says: Practice by means of such confidence!

4. The Lama Gongdü version differs by more than just a few words here: These secret words of Samantabhadra are not common knowledge for everyone. All people who possess the powerful yearning of devotion naturally realize the expanse of wisdom mind. They thus receive the mandate of transmission without having to count [lineage masters like] beads on string. People who have neither faith nor devotion and who don't practice may chase after the nine lineages without ever possessing any lineage. Your Majesty, stabilize the powerful yearning of devotion endowed with the experience of practice within the expanse of your heart!

5. Diffusion here means to become distracted and lose mindfulness. [EPK]

6. Meaning the reincarnation of the princess. He is identified as being Pema Ledrel Tsal (padma las 'brel rtsal) (1291-1315).

7. Enlightenment without remainder often means the attainment of the rainbow body. Alternately, it can mean realization of the awakened state free from the remainder of the five conditioned aggregates. [EPK]

8. The lifestyle of a 'hidden yogi' means to avoid making an outward display of spiritual qualities such as realization of the view or miraculous powers. [EPK]

9. Apparently a sentence or two is missing in the original manuscript. The bracketed text it mine. [EPK]

10. The three qualities of bliss, clarity and nonthought are basic attributes of the nature of mind and not pitfalls in themselves. When the attention is directed towards these qualities, apprehends them and becomes suffused with them as an 'experience,' as

something worthy to pursue and maintain, a subtle attachment is formed; it is this subtle fascination which is a direct cause for further samsaric existence. *Tulku Urgyen Rinpoche*

11. Same as the seven branches: prostrating, making offerings, confessing, rejoicing, requesting to turn the Wheel of the Dharma, beseeching not to pass into nirvana, and dedicating the merit for the welfare of all beings.

12. Cutting through in this case refers to the practice of Chö, cutting attachment to possessions, body and ego. [EPK]

13. This is usually mentioned as lasting for three and a half days. The old way of counting uses half-days of twelve hours. [EPK]

14. Ignorance, formation, consciousness, name-and-form, sense bases, contact, sensation, and craving; the first eight of the twelve links of dependent origination. [EPK]

15. The expression 'name-and-form' refers to the five aggregates, *form* being the aggregate of forms and *name* comprising the other four: sensations, perceptions, formations, and consciousnesses. [EPK]

16. The five ordinary light-paths are mentioned in the following paragraph.

17. This instruction refers to the indivisibility of prana and dualistic mind. The energy currents in the body and the flow of conceptual thinking are deeply interrelated. [EPK]

18. Tulku Urgyen Rinpoche explains that the pig's snout is the most sensitive point on its body; hitting it there makes it immediately run away. The reactions of either guilt and suppression or of blind involvement in an emotion are both to 'club the pig's snout,' thereby losing the opportunity to recognize the emotion's nature.

19. The following lines are written in the logical style of an Indian pandita. The end result of this line of reasoning is to arrive at the conviction that the wisdom mind of the buddhas defies any thought construct we could try to pigeon-hole it into. [EPK]

20. Often the example of pressing the eye-ball and seeing two moons is used to illustrate that personal experience is not necessarily in harmony with the nature of things. [EPK]

21. Padmasambhava here plays on the phrase 'eight wordly concerns': concerns are synonymous with *dharmas*, which can also mean Dharma teachings. [EPK]

22. As opposed to a wealthy, famous or powerful man.

23. Nyang-ral Nyima Özer's terma has at this point an additional sentence: "You may have numerous queens, attendants, and subjects, but keep in mind that you must go alone at the time of death."

24. It is often mentioned in the Prajnaparamita sutras that the bodhisattva who engages in the practice of profound emptiness will encounter many difficulties so as to quickly purify his karma and progress on the path to enlightenment. [EPK]

25. The Rinchen Terdzö version says: Humble your competetiveness towards superiors and follow the example of noble beings.

26. The topics of knowledge traditionally include philosophy, language, logic, healing, and the arts and crafts.

27. Regarding the nine gradual vehicles in the manner of upward completeness: the principles of what should be abandoned and what should be realized in any of the eight

lower vehicles are included and therefore complete within the vehicle above it. See also 'nine vehicles' in the glossary.

28. These four lines are taken from *The Ineffable Confession of the Ultimate*, the fourth chapter on Confessing Disharmony with the Wisdom Deities, extracted from the *Tantra of the Immaculate King of Confession*.

29. The three spheres are subject, object and action, or, in the instance of giving, the thing given, the act of giving, and the recipient of the gift.

30. For 'so-and-so', substitute the name of the person for the benefit of whom the dedication is made.

31. Personal practice, service in thought, word, and deed, and providing material things.

32. The unfree states are: to be a hell-being, a hungry ghost or an animal, a barbarian, or a long-living god, to have wrong views, be deprived of a buddha, or to be a mute.

33. This means fill your treasury with the two accumulations of merit and wisdom.

34. The sixth sense object is what occurs in the field of mind: past memories and future plans, present feelings of like and dislike, etc.

35. The super-knowledges including clairvoyance, recollection of former lives, and the ability to perform smaller miracles, can become the basis of spiritual pride and the formidable seduction of being a master with many followers. [EPK]

36. Definitive meaning is the direct teachings on emptiness and luminosity, as opposed to the 'expedient meaning,' which leads gradually to the definitive meaning.

37. The Mahayana resolve is the bodhisattva's vow to attain enlightenment for the welfare of all sentient beings.

SOURCES

꧁꧂

Chapter 1 — The Jewel Spike Testament: From the Kadag Rangjung Rangshar section of the Gongpa Sangtal, Volume IV (HRIH), pgs. 55-74. Tibetan title: ZHAL CHEMS RIN CHEN GZER BU🙙

Chapter 2 — Advice to Trisong Deutsen: Rinchen Terdzö edition, pgs. 180-191.

Chapter 3 — No Conflict between the Lesser and Greater Vehicles: From Rinchen Terdzö, Volume I; Section 4 of the Martri (pgs. 200-203).

Chapter 4 — The Golden Rosary of Nectar: Tibetan title: ZHUS LEN BDUD RTSI GSER PHRENG BZHUGS LAGS SO🙙

Chapter 5 — Songs to the 25 Disciples: Songs of pith instruction to each of the 25 close disciples, 48th chapter in Tongwa Dönden, page 139b. The same songs are found in the Prophecies from Lama Gongdü, pgs. 216-222. Prophesies from Lama Gongdü. Tibetan title: BLA MA DGONGS PA 'DUS PA LAS, MA 'ONG LUNG BSTAN GSANG BA'I DKAR CHAG BKOD PA'I LUNG BSTAN BKA' RGYA🙙

Chapter 6 — The Treasury of Precious Jewels to Dispel Hindrances, Replies to Questions from Yeshe Tsogyal: From the Kadag Rangjung Rangshar section, Volume IV (HRIH) of the Gongpa Sangtal, chapter 13/PO ,pgs. 261-320.. Tibetan title: GEGS SEL NOR BU RIN PO CHE'I MDZOD; MTSHO RGYAL ZHUS LAN🙙

Chapter 7 — Advice on How to Practice the Dharma: Rinchen Terdzö, Vol. "I", pgs. 230-254. Corresponds roughly to Lama Gongdü Vol. CA, pgs. 842-867.

Chapter 8 — Pointing the Staff at the Old Man: Rinchen Terdzö pgs. 463-467.

Chapter 9 — Oral Advice on Practice: From Lama Gongdü, Vol. CA, pg. 842. Corresponds to Rinchen Terdzö, Vol. I, pgs. 230-254. Tibetan title: SPYOD PA'I ZHAL GYIS

GDAMS PA࿊

Chapter 10 — The Wishfulfilling Gem of Dedication: From Lama Gongdü Vol. GA, pgs. 55-72. Tibetan title: BLA MA DGONGS PA 'DUS PA LAS: BSNGO BA NOR BU BSAM 'PHEL ZHES BYA BA BZHUGS SO࿊

Chapter 11 — A Spur Towards Spiritual Practice: A spur towards spiritual practice through the expedient meaning. A collection from Tongwa Dönden.

Chapter 12 — The Aspiration of the Vajradhatu Mandala: Found in both the Rinchen Terdzö and Chokling Tersar collections of terma treasures.

Glossary — The glossary draws on the following sources: oral teachings from Chökyi Nyima Rinpoche, Tulku Urgyen Rinpoche and Tulku Pema Wangyal; glossaries from our previous publications; notes compiled over the years by Matthieu Ricard; notes from Peter Roberts. For details of the twenty-five disciples of Padmasambhava I am also indebted to Tulku Thondup's *Tantric Tradition of the Nyingmapa* (Buddhayana 1984), and H.H. Dudjom Rinpoche's *The Nyingma School, its History and Fundamentals* (Wisdom Publications), translated by Gyurme Dorje and Matthew Kapstein.

GLOSSARY

❧

25 ATTRIBUTES OF FRUITION ('bras chos nyer lnga). The five kayas, fivefold speech, five wisdoms, five qualities, and five activities. Also called the 'continuity adorned with inexhaustible body, speech, mind, qualities, and activities.'

ABHIDHARMA (chos mngon pa). One of the three parts of the Tripitaka, the Words of the Buddha. Systematic teachings on metaphysics focusing on developing discriminating knowledge by analyzing elements of experience and investigating the nature of existing things.

ABHIDHARMA PITAKA (chos mngon pa'i sde snod). The 'Collection of Abhidharma Teachings.' See under 'Tripitaka.'

ABHISAMBODHIKAYA (mngon par byang chub pa'i sku). The fifth of the five kayas of buddhahood, defined by Jamgön Kongtrül in his *Treasury of Knowledge* as 'manifold manifestation in accordance with the karma of those to be influenced, without departing from dharmakaya, that (appears) because the (other four kayas are) spontaneously complete within awareness wisdom.'

ACCOMPLISHMENT. 1) (dngos grub, Skt. siddhi). The attainment resulting from Dharma practice usually referring to the 'supreme accomplishment' of complete enlightenment. It can also mean the 'common accomplishments,' eight mundane accomplishments such as clairvoyance, clairaudiance, flying in the sky, becoming invisible, everlasting youth, or powers of transmutation. The most eminent attainments on the path are, however, renunciation, compassion, unshakable faith and realization of the correct view. See also 'supreme and common accomplishments.' 2) (sgrub pa). See also 'approach and accomplishment.'

ACCUMULATION (tshogs). Provisions for the path. See 'two accumulations.'

AKANISHTHA ('og min). The 'highest;' the realm of Vajradhara, the enlightened sphere the dharmakaya buddha. Often used as a synonym for 'dharmadhatu.'

ALL-GROUND (kun gzhi, alaya). Literally, the 'foundation of all things.' The basis of mind and both pure and impure phenomena. This word has different meanings in different con-

156

texts and should be understood accordingly. Sometimes it is synonymous with buddha nature or dharmakaya, the recognition of which is the basis for all pure phenomena; other times, as in the case of the 'ignorant all-ground,' it refers to a neutral state of dualistic mind that has not been embraced by innate wakefulness and thus is the basis for samsaric experience.

AMRITA (bdud rtsi). Same as 'Nectar Quality,' the heruka of the ratna family among the Eight Sadhana Teachings and the tantric teachings connected with that deity.

AMRITA AND RAKTA (sman rak). Two types of blessed substance used on the shrine in Vajrayana rituals.

ANANDA (kun dga' bo). One of the ten close disciples of the Buddha; the Buddha's personal attendant, who recited the sutras at the First Council and served as the second patriarch in the oral transmission of the Dharma.

ANU YOGA (rjes su mal 'byor). The second of the Three Inner Tantras, Maha, Anu and Ati. It emphasizes knowledge (*prajna*) rather than means (*upaya*) and the completion stage rather than the development stage. The view of Anu Yoga is that liberation is attained through growing accustomed to the insight into the nondual nature of space and wisdom. The Anu Yoga mandala is regarded as contained within the vajra body. Anu means 'subsequent.'

APERTURE OF BRAHMA (tshangs bug). The opening at the top of the head, eight fingers above the hairline.

APPROACH AND ACCOMPLISHMENT (bsnyen sgrub). Two aspects of sadhana practice, in particular, phases in the recitation stage according to Mahayoga Tantra.

ASURA CAVE (a su ra'i brag phug). The cave where Guru Rinpoche subdued the evil forces of Nepal through the practice of Vajra Kilaya. Situated near Pharping in the Kathmandu Valley.

ATI YOGA (shin tu mal 'byor). The third of the Three Inner Tantras. According to Jamgön Kongtrül the First, it emphasizes the view that liberation is attained through growing accustomed to insight into the nature of primordial enlightenment, free from accepting and rejecting, hope and fear. The more common word for Ati Yoga nowadays is 'Dzogchen,' the Great Perfection. Ati means 'supreme.'

AWAKENED MIND (byang chub kyi sems, bodhichitta). See under 'bodhichitta.'

BARCHEY KÜNSEL (bar chad kun sel). See under 'Tukdrub Barchey Künsel.'

BARDO (bar do, antarabhava). 'Intermediate state.' Usually refers to the period between death and the next rebirth. For details of the four bardos, see *Mirror of Mindfulness* and *Bardo Guidebook*, Rangjung Yeshe Publications.

BHIKSHU (dge slong). A practitioner who has renounced worldly life and taken the pledge to observe the 253 precepts of a fully ordained monk in order to attain liberation from samsara.

BHUMI (sa). The bodhisattva levels; the ten stages a bodhisattva proceeds through on the quest for complete and perfect enlightenment. These ten stages correspond to the last three of the five paths of Mahayana. See also 'ten bhumis.'

BLISS, CLARITY, AND NONTHOUGHT (bde gsal mi rtog pa). Three temporary meditation experiences. Fixation on them plants the seeds for rebirth in the three realms of samsara. Without fixation, they are adornments of the three kayas.

BLISSFUL REALM (bde ba can, Sukhavati). The pure land of Buddha Amitabha in which a practitioner can take rebirth during the bardo of becoming through a combination of pure faith, sufficient merit, and one-pointed determination.

BODHICHITTA (byang sems, byang chub kyi sems). 'Awakened state of mind,' 'enlightened attitude.' 1) The aspiration to attain enlightenment for the sake of all beings. 2) In the context of Dzogchen, the innate wakefulness of awakened mind; synonymous with nondual awareness.

BODHISATTVA (byang chub sems dpa'). Someone who has developed bodhichitta, the aspiration to attain enlightenment in order to benefit all sentient beings. A practitioner of the Mahayana path; especially a noble bodhisattva who has attained the first level.

BODHISATTVA PRECEPTS (byang sdom). According to the system of Nagarjuna, the Chariot of the Profound View, the precepts are to refrain from the following: to steal the funds of the Three Jewels; to commit the act of forsaking the Dharma; to punish or cause to lose the precepts etc. people who possess or have lapsed from the trainings; to commit the five acts with immediate result; to violate the five definite precepts for a king, such as keeping wrong views and so forth; to violate the five definitive precepts for a minister such as destroying a village, a valley, a city, a district, or a country; to give premature teachings on emptiness to people who haven't trained in the Mahayana; to aspire towards the shravakas of the Hinayana after having reached the Mahayana; to train in the Mahayana after forsaking the Individual Liberation; to disparage the Hinayana; to praise oneself and disparage others; to be highly hypocritical for the sake of honor and gain; to let a monk receive punishment and be humiliated; to harm others by bribing a king or a minister in order to punish them; to give the food of a renunciant meditator to a reciter of scriptures and thus causing obstacles for the cultivation of shamatha. The eighty subsidiary infractions are to forsake the happiness of another being and so forth. According to the system of Asanga, the Chariot of the Vast Conduct, the precepts for the bodhichitta of aspiration are as follows: to never forsake sentient beings, to remember the benefits of bodhichitta, to gather the accumulations, to exert oneself in training in bodhichitta, as well as to adopt and avoid the eight black and white deeds. The four precepts for the bodhichitta of application are (to avoid the following): 1) out of desire, to have exceeding attachment to honor and gain and to praise oneself and disparage others, 2) out of stinginess, to refrain from giving material things, Dharma teachings and wealth to others, 3) out of anger, to harm others and be unforgiving when offered an apology, 4) out of stupidity, to pretend that indolence is Dharma and to teach that to others. The 46 minor infractions are to refrain from making offerings to the Three Jewels and so forth. The four black deeds are to deceive a venerable person, to cause someone to regret what is not regrettable, to disparage a sublime person, and to deceive sentient beings. The four white are their opposites.

BUDDHAHOOD (sangs rgyas). The perfect and complete enlightenment dwelling in neither samsara nor nirvana; the state of having eradicated all obscurations, endowed with the wisdom of seeing the nature of things as it is and with the wisdom of perceiving all that exists.

BURNT OFFERINGS (gsur). Smoke produced by burning flour mixed with pure food and sacred substances. This smoke, offered during a meditation on Avalokiteshvara, the bodhisattva of compassion, can nourish the bardo consciousness as well as hungry ghosts.

CAUSAL AND RESULTANT VEHICLES (rgyu dang 'bras bu'i theg pa). The teachings of Hinayana and Mahayana that regard the practices of the path as the causes for attaining the fruition of liberation and enlightenment and the Vajrayana system of taking fruition as the path by regarding buddhahood as inherently present and the path as the act of uncovering the basic state. The great master Longchenpa defined them as follows: "The causal vehicles are so called because of accepting a sequence of cause and effect, asserting that buddhahood is attained by increasing the qualities of the nature of the sugata essence, which is merely present as a seed, through the circumstance of the two accumulations. The resultant vehicles are so called because of asserting that the basis for purification is the (sugata) essence endowed with qualities that are spontaneously present as a natural possession in sentient beings, just as the sun is endowed with rays of light; that the objects of purification are the temporary defilements of the eight collections (of consciousnesses), like the sky being (temporarily) obscured by clouds; and that one realizes the result of purification, the primordially present nature, by means of that which purifies, the paths of ripening and liberation. Besides this, there is no difference (between the two) in sequence or quality."

CENTRAL CHANNEL (dbu ma, avadhuti). The central subtle channel within the body, running from the base of the spine to the crown of the head.

CHANNEL (rtsa). See 'nadi.'

CHETSÜN NYINGTIG (lce btsun snying tig). One of the most important Dzogchen instructions, based on a transmission from Vimalamitra. Jamyang Khyentse had a vision of Chetsün Senge Wangchuk which inspired him to write the precious teaching known as *Chetsün Nyingtig*. Senge Wangchuk (11th-12th century) is among the lineage gurus in the Nyingtig transmission, which he received from his root guru, Dangma Lhüngyal, as well as directly from Vimalamitra. As a result of his high level of realization, his physical body disappeared in rainbow light at the time of death. In a later reincarnation as Jamyang Khyentse Wangpo, he remembered the Dzogchen teachings which Senge Wangchuk had transmitted to the dakini Palgyi Lodrö and wrote them down as the terma *Chetsün Nyingtig*, the 'Heart Essence of Chetsün.'

CHÖ (gcod). Literally 'cutting.' A system of practices based on Prajnaparamita and set down by the Indian siddha Phadampa Sangye and the Tibetan female teacher Machig Labdrön for the purpose of cutting through the four Maras and ego-clinging. One of the Eight Practice Lineages of Buddhism in Tibet.

CHOKGYUR LINGPA (mchog gyur gling pa). (1829-1870). A treasure revealer and contemporary of Jamyang Khyentse Wangpo and Jamgön Kongtrül. Regarded as one of the major tertöns in Tibetan history, his termas are widely practiced by both the Kagyü and Nyingma schools. For more details see *The Life and Teachings of Chokgyur Lingpa* (Rangjung Yeshe Publications). Chokgyur Lingpa means 'Sanctuary of Eminence.'

CLARITY (gsal ba). See 'bliss, clarity and nonthought.'

COEMERGENT IGNORANCE (lhan cig skyes pa'i ma rig pa). Ignorance that is coemergent with our innate nature and remains present as the potential for confusion to arise when meeting with the right conditions.

COGNITIVE OBSCURATION (shes bya'i sgrib pa). The subtle obscuration of holding on to the concepts of subject, object and action. It is temporarily purified in the moment of recognizing the nature of mind, and utterly purified through the vajra-like samadhi at the end of the tenth bhumi.

COMPLETION STAGE (rdzogs rim). See 'development and completion.'

CONCEPTUAL IGNORANCE (kun brtags kyi ma rig pa). In Vajrayana, conceptual ignorance is the mind apprehending itself as subject and object; conceptual thinking. In the Sutra system, conceptual ignorance means superimposed or 'learned' wrong views; gross general beliefs that obscure the nature of things.

CONDITIONED VIRTUE (zag bcas kyi dge ba). Spiritual practice in which a dualistic point of reference is used. Includes the *preliminaries*, seven branches and so forth. Unconditioned virtue is the recognition of buddha nature, often called 'threefold purity.' These two aspects of virtue gather the *two accumulations*, remove the *two obscurations*, manifest the *twofold knowledge*, and actualize the *two kayas*.

CONSTRUCTS (spros pa). Any mental formulation. A conceptual fabrication that is not innate to the nature of mind.

DAKINI (mkha' 'gro ma). 1) Spiritual beings who fulfill the enlightened activities; female tantric deities who protect and serve the Buddhist doctrine and practitioners. Also one of the 'Three Roots.' 2) Female enlightened practitioner of Vajrayana.

DAKINI TEACHINGS: *Padmasambhava's Oral Instructions to Lady Tsogyal* (Shambhala Publications). A collection of the great master's advice from the revelations of Nyang Ral, Sangye Lingpa and Dorje Lingpa. Covers the topics of taking refuge, bodhisattva vows, the vajra master, yidam practice, retreat, and the qualities of fruition.

DATHIM (brda' thim). Literally 'sign dissolved,' this word often occurs at the end of a terma.

DAKINI (mkha' 'gro ma). 1) Spiritual beings who fulfill the enlightened activities; female tantric deities who protect and serve the Buddhist doctrine and practitioners. Also one of the 'Three Roots.' 2) Enlightened female practitioner of Vajrayana.

DENMA TSEMANG (ldan ma rtse mang). Important early Tibetan translator of the Tripitaka. Extremely well-versed in writing, his style of calligraphy has continued to the present day. Having received Vajrayana transmission from Padmasambhava, he had realization and achieved perfect recall. He is said to be the chief scribe who wrote down many termas, including the *Assemblage of Sugatas*, connected to the Eight Sadhana Teachings.

DEPENDENT ORIGINATION (rten cing 'brel bar 'byung ba). The natural law that all phenomena arise 'dependent upon' their own causes 'in connection with' their individual conditions. The fact that no phenomena appear without a cause and none are made by an uncaused creator. Everything arises exclusively due to and dependent upon the coincidence of causes and conditions without which they cannot possibly appear.

DEVELOPMENT AND COMPLETION (bskyed rdzogs). The two main aspects, 'means and knowledge,' of Vajrayana practice. Briefly stated, development stage means positive mental fabrication while completion stage means resting in the unfabricated nature of mind. The essence of the development stage is 'pure perception' or 'sacred outlook,' which means to perceive sights, sounds and thoughts as deity, mantra and wisdom. 'Completion stage with marks' means yogic practices such as *tummo*, inner heat. 'Completion stage without marks' is the practice of Dzogchen and Mahamudra.

DEVELOPMENT STAGE (bskyed rim). See 'development and completion.'

DHARMA PROTECTOR (chos skyong). Nonhumans who vow to protect and guard the teachings of the Buddha and its followers. Dharma protectors can be either 'mundane' (virtuous samsaric beings) or 'wisdom Dharma protectors' (emanations of buddhas or bodhisattvas).

DHARMADHATU (chos kyi dbyings). The 'realm of phenomena;' the suchness in which emptiness and dependent origination are inseparable. The nature of mind and phenomena which lies beyond arising, dwelling and ceasing.

DHARMAKAYA (chos sku). The first of the three kayas, which is devoid of constructs, like space. The 'body' of enlightened qualities. Should be understood individually according to ground, path and fruition.

DHARMARAJA, THE LORD OF DEATH (gshin rje chos rgyal). Our mortality; a personification of impermanence and the unfailing law of cause and effect.

DHARMATA (chos nyid). The innate nature of phenomena and mind.

DHYANA (bsam gtan). The state of concentrated mind and also the name for god realms produced through such mental concentration. See also under 'four dhyana states.'

DISTURBING EMOTIONS (nyon mongs pa). The five poisons of desire, anger, delusion, pride, and envy which tire, disturb, and torment one's mind. The perpetuation of these disturbing emotions is one of the main causes of samsaric existence.

DÖN (gdon). A negative force; a type of evil spirit.

DORJE DUDJOM OF NANAM (sna nam pa rdo rje bdud 'joms). One of king Trisong Deutsen's ministers, sent to Nepal to invite Padmasambhava to Tibet. A *mantrika* who had reached perfection in the two stages of development and completion, he could fly with the speed of the wind and traverse solid matter. Rigdzin Gödem (1337-1408) and Pema Trinley (1641-1718), the great vidyadhara of Dorje Drak monastery in central Tibet, are both considered reincarnations of Dorje Dudjom. Dorje Dudjom means 'Indestructible Subduer of Mara.'

DRENPA NAMKHA (dran pa nam mkha'). Tibetan translator and disciple of Padmasambhava, originally an influential Bönpo priest. Later he studied with Padmasambhava and also learned translation. He is said to have tamed a wild yak simply by a threatening gesture. He offered numerous Bönpo teachings to Padmasambhava who then concealed them as terma treasures. Drenpa Namkha means 'Space of Mindfulness.'

DRIB (grib). Defilement, obscuration caused by contact with impure people or their things.

DRUBCHEN CEREMONY (sgrub chen). Great accomplishment practice; a sadhana practice undertaken by a group of people which goes on uninterruptedly for seven days.

DZONGSAR KHYENTSE CHÖKYI LODRÖ (rdzong gsar mkhyen brtse chos kyi blo gros). One of five reincarnations of Jamyang Khyentse Wangpo. He was a great master upholding the Rimey (nonsectarian) tradition, as well as being one of the two main root gurus of His Holiness Dilgo Khyentse. His three reincarnations live presently at Bir, Himachal Pradesh; in Dordogne, France; and in Boudhanath, Nepal. Dzongsar means 'New Castle,' Khyentse means 'Loving Wisdom,' and Chökyi Lodrö means 'Intellect of the Dharma.'

EARLY TRANSLATIONS (snga 'gyur). A synonym for the Old School, the Nyingma tradition. The teachings translated before the great translator Rinchen Sangpo, during the reigns of the Tibetan kings Trisong Deutsen and Ralpachen.

EARTH TERMA (sa gter). A revelation based on physical substance, often in the form of dakini script, a vajra, a statue, etc. Compare with 'mind terma.'

EIGHT COLLECTIONS OF CONSCIOUSNESSES (mam shes tshogs brgyad): the all-ground consciousness, the defiled mental consciousness, the mental cognition, and the cognitions of eye, ear, nose, tongue, and body.

EIGHT LINGPAS (gling pa brgyad). Sangye, Dorje, Rinchen, Padma, Ratna, Kunkyong, Dongag and Tennyi Lingpa.

EIGHT SADHANA TEACHINGS (sgrub pa bka' brgyad). Eight chief yidam deities of Mahayoga and their corresponding tantras and sadhanas: Manjushri Body, Lotus Speech, Vishuddha Mind, Nectar Quality, Kilaya Activity, Liberating Sorcery of Mother Deities, Maledictory Fierce Mantra, and Mundane Worship. Often the name refers to a single practice involving complex mandalas with numerous deities.

EIGHT WORLDLY CONCERNS ('jig rten chos brgyad). Attachment to gain, pleasure, praise and fame, and aversion to loss, pain, blame and bad reputation.

ENHANCEMENT (bogs 'don). Various practices with the purpose of stabilizing insight. According to Tulku Urgyen Rinpoche, the main enhancement practice is the cultivation of devotion and compassion.

ESSENCE KAYA (ngo bo nyid kyi sku; Skt. svabhavikakaya). The 'essence body,' sometimes counted as the fourth kaya, and constituting the unity of the three kayas. Jamgön Kongtrül defines it as the aspect of dharmakaya which is 'the nature of all phenomena, emptiness devoid of all constructs and endowed with the characteristic of natural purity.'

ESSENCE MANTRA (snying po'i sngags). The short form of the mantra of a yidam deity as opposed to the longer dharani mantra; for example 'om mani padme hung.'

ESSENCE, NATURE, AND CAPACITY (ngo bo rang bzhin thugs rje). The three aspects of the sugata-garbha according to the Dzogchen system. Essence is the primordially pure wisdom of emptiness. The nature is the spontaneously present wisdom of cognizance. The capacity is the all-pervasive wisdom of indivisibility. This is, ultimately, the identity of the Three Roots, the Three Jewels and the three kayas.

ETERNALISM (rtag lta). The belief that there is a permanent and causeless creator of everything; in particular, that one's identity or consciousness has a concrete essence which is independent, everlasting and singular.

FATHER TANTRA (pha rgyud). One of the three aspects of Anuttara Yoga which place emphasis on the development stage.

FEAST OFFERING (tshogs kyi 'khor lo, Skt. ganachakra). A feast assembly performed by Vajrayana practitioners to accumulate merit and purify the sacred commitments.

FIVE KING-LIKE TERTÖNS (gter ston rgyal po lnga). One list of the Five Tertön Kings contains Nyang Ral Nyima Özer (1124-1192), Guru Chökyi Wangchuk (1212-1270), Dorje Lingpa (1346-1405), Pema Lingpa (1445/50-1521), and (Padma Ösel) Do-ngak Lingpa (Jamyang Khyentse Wangpo) (1820-1892). Sometimes the list also includes the great tertön Rigdzin Gödem (1337-1408).

FIVE PATHS (lam lnga). The five paths or stages on the way to enlightenment: the path of accumulation, joining, seeing, cultivation, and consummation or no more learning.

FIVE POISONS (dug lnga). Desire, anger, delusion, pride, and envy.

FORMLESS REALMS (gzugs med kyi khams). The abodes of unenlightened beings who have practiced formless meditative states, dwelling on the notions: Infinite Space, Infinite Consciousness, Nothing Whatsoever, and Neither Presence Nor Absence (of conception). These beings remain in these four subtle types of conceptual meditation for many aeons after which they again return to lower states within samsara.

FOUR DHYANA STATES OF SERENITY (snyoms 'jug gi bsam gtan bzhi). The first dhyana is a state with both concept and discernment. The second dhyana is a state without concept but with discernment. The third dhyana is a state without delight but with bliss. The fourth dhyana is a state of equanimity.

FOUR FORMLESS STATES OF SERENITY (gzugs med kyi snyoms 'jug bzhi). See 'Formless Realms.'

FOUR MODES (tshul bzhi). Four levels of meaning: the literal, the general, the hidden, and the ultimate.

FOUR ROOT PRECEPTS (rtsa ba bzhi). To refrain from killing, stealing, lying, and sexual misconduct.

FREEDOMS AND RICHES (dal 'byor). See under 'precious human body.'

FRUITION ('bras bu). The result, usually the end of a spiritual path. One of the three levels of enlightenment of a shravaka, pratyekabuddha or bodhisattva. In Mahayana the state of complete and perfect buddhahood; in Vajrayana the 'unified state of a vajra-holder,' in this book expressed as the '25 attributes of fruition.' See also 'view, meditation, action and fruition.'

GARAB DORJE (dga' rab rdo rje, Skt. Surati Vajra, Prahevajra, Pramoda Vajra). The incarnation of Semlhag Chen, a god who earlier had been empowered by the buddhas. Immaculately conceived, his mother was a nun, the daughter of King Uparaja (Dhahenatalo or Indrabhuti) of Uddiyana. Garab Dorje received all the tantras, scriptures and oral instructions of Dzogchen from Vajrasattva and Vajrapani in person and became the first human vidyadhara in the Dzogchen lineage. Having reached the state of complete enlightenment through the effortless Great Perfection, Garab Dorje transmitted the teachings to his retinue of exceptional beings. Manjushrimitra is regarded as his chief disciple. Padmasambhava is also known to have received the transmission of the Dzogchen tantras directly from Garab Dorje's wisdom form. Garab Dorje means 'Indestructible joy.'

GLORIOUS MOUNTAIN IN CHAMARA / GLORIOUS COPPER COLORED

MOUNTAIN (rnga g.yab zangs mdog dpal ri). The terrestrial pure land of Guru Rinpoche situated on the subcontinent Chamara to the south-east of the Jambu Continent. Chamara is the central of a configuration of nine islands inhabited by savage rakshas. In the middle of Chamara rises the majestic red colored mountain into the skies. On its summit lies the magical palace Lotus Light, manifested from the natural expression of primordial wakefulness. Here resides Padmasambhava in an indestructible bodily form transcending birth and death for as long as samsara continues and through which he incessantly brings benefit to beings through magical emanations of his body, speech and mind.

GONGPA SANGTAL (dgongs pa zang thal). A tantric scripture in five volumes concealed by Guru Rinpoche and revealed by Rigdzin Gödem, the master who founded the Jangter tradition of the Nyingma school. Contains the renowned 'Aspiration of Samantabhadra.' Gongpa Sangtal means 'Unimpeded realization,' and is an abbreviation of 'Showing Directly the Realization of Samantabhadra' (kun tu bzang po'i dgongs pa zang thal du bstan pa).

GREAT CAVE OF PURI / CRYSTAL CAVE OF PURI PHUGMOCHE (spu ri phug mo che shel gyi brag phug). The treasure site of Sangye Lingpa in the Puwo district bordering Assam, where he revealed the Lama Gongdü cycle.

GREAT PERFECTION (rdzogs pa chen po, Skt. mahasandhi). The third of the Three Inner Tantras of the Nyingma School. The Great Perfection is the ultimate of all the 84,000 profound and extensive sections of the Dharma, the realization of Buddha Samantabhadra, exactly as it is. See also 'Dzogchen' or 'Ati Yoga.'

GUHYASAMAJA (gsang ba 'dus pa). Literally, 'Assembly of Secrets.' One of the major tantras and yidams of the New School.

GURU CHÖWANG (gu ru chos dbang). One of the Five Tertön Kings. (1212-1270). For details, see the H.H. Dudjom Rinpoche's *The Nyingma Lineage, its History and Fundamentals*, Wisdom Publications. Guru Chöwang means 'Master Lord of the Dharma.'

GYALPO SPIRITS (rgyal po). A type of mischievous spirit, sometimes counted among the 'eight classes of gods and demons.' When subdued by a great master, they can also act as guardians of the Buddhadharma.

GYALWA CHO-YANG OF NGANLAM (ngan lam rgyal ba mchog dbyangs). A close disciple of Guru Rinpoche who attained accomplishment through the practice of Hayagriva and was later incarnated as the Karmapas. Born into the Nganlam clan in the Phen Valley, he took ordination from Shantarakshita in the first group of seven Tibetan monks. It is said that he kept his vows with utmost purity. Having received the transmission of Hayagriva from Padmasambhava, he practiced in solitude and reached the level of a vidyadhara. Gyalwa Cho-yang means 'Sublime voice of victory.'

GYALWA JANGCHUB OF LASUM (la gsum rgyal ba byang chub). One of the first seven Tibetans to receive full ordination as a monk by Shantarakshita, he was exceedingly intelligent, visited India several times and translated many sacred scriptures. A close disciple of Padmasambhava, he attained siddhi and could fly through the sky. Rigdzin Kunzang Sherab, the founder of the great Palyül Monastery in Kham, is considered one of his reincarnations. Gyalwa Jangchub means 'Victorious enlightenment.'

GYALWEY LODRÖ OF DREY ('bre rgyal ba'i blo gros). Beginning as Gönpo, a trusted attendant of Trisong Deutsen, he became one of the first Tibetans to take ordination, taking the name Gyalwey Lodrö, Victorious Intelligence. He became erudite in translation and attained accomplishment after receiving transmission from Hungkara in India. It is said that he visited the land of Yama, the Lord of the Dead, and saved his mother from the hell realms. After receiving teachings from Padmasambhava, he performed the feat of transforming a zombie into gold, some of which was later revealed in terma treasures. He achieved the vidyadhara level of longevity and is reputed to have lived until the era of Rongzom Pandita Chökyi Sangpo (rong zom chos kyi bzang po) (1012-1088), to whom he gave teachings. Gyalwey Lodrö means 'Victorious wisdom.'

HAYAGRIVA (rta mgrin). Tantric deity shown with a horse's head within his flaming hair; wrathful aspect of Buddha Amitabha. Here identical with Padma Heruka, Lotus Speech, among the Eight Sadhana Teachings.

HEARING LINEAGE (nyan brgyud). The lineage of oral teachings from master to disciple as distinct from scriptural lineage of textual transmission. The Hearing Lineage emphasizes the key points of oral instruction rather than elaborate philosophical learning.

HEART ESSENCE (snying thig). In general identical with the Instruction Section, the third of three division of Dzogchen. In particular it refers to the Innermost Unexcelled Cycle of Heart Essence (yang gsang bla na med pa'i snying thig gi skor), the fourth of the four divisions of the Instruction Section according to the arrangement of Shri Singha. All lineages of the Innermost Essence passed through Shri Singha and continued in Tibet through his personal disciples, Padmasambhava and Vimalamitra. In the 14th century these two lineages passed through Rangjung Dorje, the third Karmapa, and his close Dharma friend Longchen Rabjam (1308-1363), the latter of which systematized these teachings in his great body of writings. The Nyingtig teachings have also appeared through many other lines of transmission; for instance, each major tertön reveals an independent cycle of Dzogchen instructions. The practice of the innermost Heart Essence is continued to this very day.

HEAT OF SAMADHI (ting nge 'dzin gyi drod). Sign of progress or accomplishment in meditation.

HIGHER PERCEPTIONS (mngon par shes pa). See 'superknowledges.'

HINAYANA (theg pa dman pa). The vehicles focused on contemplation of the four noble truths and the twelve links of dependent origination, the practice of which brings liberation from cyclic existence. When used in a derogative sense, the Hinayana attitude refers to the narrow pursuit of a spiritual path simply for the sake of individual liberation rather than for the enlightenment of all sentient beings.

HUNDRED SYLLABLE MANTRA (yig brgya). The mantra of the buddha Vajrasattva consisting of one hundred syllables.

IGNORANT ALL-GROUND / IGNORANT ASPECT OF THE ALL-GROUND (kun gzhi ma rig pa'i cha). Synonymous with coemergent ignorance.

INNATE NATURE (chos nyid). See under 'dharmata.'

INNERMOST UNEXCELLED CYCLE OF THE GREAT PERFECTION (rdzogs pa chen po yang gsang bla na med pa'i skor).

JAMGÖN KONGTRÜL ('jam mgon kong sprul). (1813-1899). Also known as Lodrö Thaye, Yönten Gyamtso, Padma Garwang and by his tertön name Padma Tennyi Yungdrung Lingpa. He was one of the most prominent Buddhist masters in the 19th century and placed special focus upon a non-sectarian attitude. Renowned as an accomplished master, scholar and writer, he authored more than 100 volumes of scriptures. The most well known are his Five Treasuries, among which are the 63 volumes of the Rinchen Terdzö, the terma literature of the one hundred great tertöns.

JAMYANG KHYENTSE WANGPO ('jam dbyangs mkhyen brtse'i dbang po). (1820-1892). A great master of the last century. He was the last of the Five Great Tertöns and was regarded as the combined reincarnation of Vimalamitra and King Trisong Deutsen. He became the master and teacher of all the Buddhist schools of Tibet and the founder of the Rimey movement. There are ten volumes of his works in addition to his termas. Jamyang means 'Manjushri, gentle melodiousness,' Khyentse Wangpo means 'Lord of loving wisdom.'

JNANA KUMARA OF NYAG (gnyag jna na ku ma ra, ye shes gzhon nu). Jnana Kumara means 'Youthful Wakefulness.' Early Tibetan monk and expert translator who received the Four Great Rivers of Transmission from Padmasambhava, Vimalamitra, Vairochana and Yudra Nyingpo. He worked closely with Vimalamitra in translating tantras of Mahayoga and Ati Yoga. He is also known as Nyag Lotsawa and by his secret initiation name Drimey Dashar, 'Flawless Moonlight.' His initiation flower, along with Trisong Deutsen's, fell on Chemchok Heruka. Subsequently, he received the transmission of Nectar Medicine from Padmasambhava. He practiced in the Crystal Cave of Yarlung, where he drew water from solid rock; it is said this water still flows today. Among his later incarnations is Dabzang Rinpoche, a 19th-century contemporary of Jamgön Kongtrül the First. Jnana Kumara means 'Youthful Wakefulness.'

JOYOUS BHUMI (sa rab tu dga' ba). The first of ten bodhisattva stages; liberation from samsara and realization of the truth of reality.

KADAG RANGJUNG RANGSHAR (ka dag rang byung rang shar). The title of one of the five volumes contained in *Gongpa Sangtal*. Kadag Rangjung Rangshar means 'self-existing and self-manifest primordial purity.'

KARMA PAKSHI (karma pakshi). (1204-1283). The second in the line of Karmapa incarnations and is regarded as the first recognized Tibetan tulku. The name Pakshi is Mongolian for 'master,' a title he became renowned under after being given a high religious position by the Mongolian emperor. Among his disciples is the great siddha Orgyenpa Rinchen Pal (1230-1309).

KAWA PALTSEK (ska ba dpal brtsegs). Direct disciple of both Padmasambhava and Shantarakshita; important contributor to the translation of the Tibetan Tripitaka and the Nyingma Gyübum. Born in Phen Valley, he became an eminent translator in accordance with a prophecy by Padmasambhava, and was among the first seven Tibetan monks ordained by Shantarakshita. He received Vajrayana teachings from the great master Padma and attained unimpeded clairvoyance. Kawa is a place name and Paltsek means 'Mountain of resplendence.'

KAYAS (sku). 'Body' in the sense of a body or embodiment of numerous qualities. When speaking of two kayas: dharmakaya and rupakaya. The three kayas are dharmakaya, sambhogakaya and nirmanakaya. See also 'three kayas.'

KHANDRO NYINGTIG (mkha' 'gro snying thig). Khandro Nyingtig means 'Heart Essence of the Dakinis.' A profound collection of Dzogchen teachings transmitted through Padmasambhava to Princess Pema Sal. Is included within the famous *Nyingtig Yabshi*.

KHENPO (mkhan po). A title for one who has completed the major course of studies of about ten years' duration of the traditional branches of Buddhist philosophy, logic, Vinaya and so forth. Can also refer to the abbot of a monastery or the preceptor from whom one receives ordination.

KHENPO NGAKCHUNG ALIAS NGAWANG PALSANG (mkhan po ngag dbang dpal bzang). (1879-1941). A khenpo at Katok and a very important reviver of the scholastic lineage of expounding the Dzogchen scriptures. Considered to be incarnation of both Vimalamitra and Longchenpa. Chadral Sangye Dorje is one of his last living disciples.

KILAYA (Skt., phur pa). The tantras about and the tantric deity Vajra Kilaya.

KÖNCHOK CHIDÜ (dkon mchog spyi 'dus). The 'Embodiment of the Precious Ones.' A terma cycle revealed by the great Jatsön Nyingpo (1585-1656) focused on Padmasambhava. He transmitted this set of teachings first to Düdül Dorje (1615-1672). Large portions of this material are translated into English by Peter Roberts.

KÖNCHOK JUNGNEY OF LANGDRO (lang gro dkon mchog 'byung gnas). At first a minister at the court of Trisong Deutsen, he later became one of Padmasambhava's close disciples and attained accomplishment. The great tertöns Ratna Lingpa (1403-1471) and Longsal Nyingpo (1625-1692) are considered to be among his reincarnations. Könchok Jungney means 'Source of the Precious Ones.'

KRIYA YOGA (bya ba'i mal 'byor). The first of the three outer tantras which places emphasis on cleanliness and pure conduct. The scriptures of Kriya Tantra appeared first in Varanasi.

KUNZANG TUKTIG (kun bzang thugs thig). The 'Heart Essence of Samantabhadra.' A collection of terma teachings revealed by Chokgyur Lingpa focused on the peaceful and wrathful deities.

LAMA GONGDÜ (bla ma dgongs 'dus). Cycle revealed by Sangye Lingpa (1340-96) in 18 volumes of approximately 700 pages each. Lama Gongdü means 'embodiment of the master's realization.'

LAMA SANGDÜ (bla ma gsang 'dus). A terma discovered by Guru Chöwang (1212-1270), one of the earliest and most important tertöns. It focuses on the guru principle as Padmasambhava's sambhogakaya form of the fivefold mandala of Tötreng Tsal. Lama Sangdü means 'embodiment of the master's secrets.'

LEARNING, REFLECTION AND MEDITATION (thos bsam sgom gsum). 'Learning' means receiving oral teachings and studying scriptures in order to clear away ignorance and wrong views. 'Reflection' is to eradicate uncertainty and misunderstanding through carefully thinking over the subject. 'Meditation' means to gain direct insight through applying the teachings in one's personal experience.

LOBPÖN BODHISATTVA, ALIAS SHANTARAKSHITA (zhi ba 'tsho), 'Guardian of Peace.' The Indian pandita and abbot of Vikramashila and of Samye who ordained the first Tibetan monks. He was an incarnation of the bodhisattva Vajrapani and is also known as

Khenpo Bodhisattva or Bhikshu Bodhisattva Shantarakshita. He is the founder of a philosophical school combining Madhyamika and Yogachara. This tradition was reestablished and clarified by Mipham Rinpoche in his commentary on the *Madhyamaka Lamkara*.

LOKYI CHUNGPA (lo ki chung pa). A close disciple of Padmasambhava who became a Buddhist translator while very young, hence his name. He is also known as Khyeu-chung Lotsawa, 'Boy Translator.' Among his later incarnations are the tertön Düdül Dorje (1615-1672), Dudjom Lingpa (1835-1903), and H.H. Dudjom Rinpoche, Jigdrel Yeshe Dorje (1904-1987).

LONGCHENPA ALIAS LONGCHEN RABJAM (klong chen pa, klong chen rab 'byams). (1308-1363) An incarnation of Princess Pema Sal, the daughter of King Trisong Deutsen, to whom Guru Rinpoche had entrusted his own lineage of Dzogchen known as Khandro Nyingtig. He is single-handedly regarded as the most important writer on Dzogchen teachings. His works include the Seven Great Treasuries, the Three Trilogies and his commentaries in the Nyingtig Yabshi. A more detailed account of his life and teachings is found in *Buddha Mind* by Tulku Thondup Rinpoche (Snow Lion Publications), 1989. Longchenpa means 'Great expanse.'

LORD OF DEATH (gshin rje). 1) A personification of impermanence and the unfailing law of cause and effect. 2) ('chi bdag) The demon with this name is one of the four Maras; see under 'Mara.'

LUMINOSITY ('od gsal). Literally 'free from the darkness of unknowing and endowed with the ability to cognize.' The two aspects are 'empty luminosity,' like a clear open sky, which is the cognizant quality of the nature of mind; and 'manifest luminosity,' such as five-colored lights, images, and so forth. Luminosity is the uncompounded nature present throughout all of samsara and nirvana.

MACHIG LABDRÖN (ma gcig lab sgron). (1031-1129). The great female master who set down the Chö practice, cutting through ego-clinging. Disciple and consort of the Indian master Phadampa Sangye. Machig Labdrön means 'Only Mother Lamp of Dharma.'

MAHAYANA (theg pa chen po). 'Greater vehicle.' When using the term 'greater and lesser vehicles,' Mahayana and Hinayana, Mahayana includes the tantric vehicles while Hinayana is comprised of the teachings for shravakas and pratyekabuddhas. The connotation of 'greater' or 'lesser' refers to the scope of aspiration, the methods applied and the depth of insight. Central to Mahayana practice is the bodhisattva vow to liberate all sentient beings through means and knowledge, compassion and insight into emptiness. Mahayana's two divisions are known as Mind Only and Middle Way. The sevenfold greatness of Mahayana mentioned in Maitreya's *Ornament of the Sutras* are explained by Jamgön Kongtrül in his *All-encompassing Knowledge:* "The greatness of focus on the immense collection of Mahayana teachings, the greatness of the means of accomplishing the welfare of both self and others, the greatness of wisdom that realizes the twofold egolessness, the greatness of diligent endeavor for three incalculable aeons, the greatness of skillful means such as not abandoning samsaric existence and enacting the seven unvirtuous actions of body and speech without disturbing emotions, the greatness of true accomplishment of the ten strengths, the fourfold fearlessness, and the unique qualities of the awakened ones, and the greatness of activity that is spontaneous and unceasing."

MAHAYOGA (mal 'byor chen po). The first of the 'Three Inner Tantras.' Mahayoga as scripture is divided into two parts: Tantra Section and Sadhana Section. The Tantra Section consists of the Eighteen Mahayoga Tantras while the Sadhana Section is comprised of the Eight Sadhana Teachings. Jamgön Kongtrül says in his *Treasury of Knowledge*: "Mahayoga emphasizes means (*upaya*), the development stage, and the view that liberation is attained through growing accustomed to the insight into the nature of the indivisibility of the superior two truths." The superior two truths in Mahayoga are purity and equality — the pure natures of the aggregates, elements and sense factors are the male and female buddhas and bodhisattvas. At the same time, everything that appears and exists is of the equal nature of emptiness.

MAMO (ma mo). Abbreviation of 'Mundane Mother Deities' ('jig rten ma mo). One of the Eight Sadhana Teachings. Female divinities manifested out of dharmadhatu but appearing in ways that correspond to mundane appearances through the interrelationship between the mundane world and the channels, winds, and essences within our body. They have both an ultimate and relative aspect. The chief figure in this mandala is Chemchok Heruka, the wrathful form of Buddha Samantabhadra in the form known as Ngöndzok Gyalpo, the King of True Perfection.

MANDALA (dkyil 'khor). 1) 'Center and surrounding.' Usually a deity along with its surrounding environment. A mandala is a symbolic, graphic representation of a tantric deity's realm of existence. 2) A mandala offering is an offering visualized as the entire universe, as well as the arrangement of offerings in tantric ritual.

MANDARAVA (man da ra ba me tog). Princess of Zahor and close disciple of Guru Rinpoche. One of his five main consorts. Her name refers to the coral tree, Erythrina Indica, one of the five trees of paradise, which has brilliant scarlet flowers. She is said to be identical with the dakini Niguma and the yogini by the name Adorned with Human Bone Ornaments. In *The Precious Garland of Lapis Lazuli*, Jamgön Kongtrül says, "Born as the daughter of Vihardhara, the king of Zahor, and Queen Mohauki accompanied by miraculous signs, (and because of her great beauty), many kings from India and China vied to take her as their bride. Nevertheless, she had an unshakable renunciation and entered the gate of the Dharma. Padmasambhava perceived that she was to be his disciple and accepted her as his spiritual consort, but the king, fearing that his bloodline would be contaminated, had the master burned alive. When Padmasambhava showed the miracle of transforming the mass of fire into a lake, the king gained faith and without hesitation offered his entire kingdom and the princess. When the king requested teachings, Padmasambhava showered upon twenty-one disciples the great rain of the Dharma by transmitting the tantras, scriptures and oral instructions of Kadü Chökyi Gyamtso, the Dharma Ocean Embodying All Teachings. Thus, the master established the king and his ministers on the vidyadhara levels. Guru Rinpoche accepted her as his consort and in Maratika, the Cave of Bringing Death to and End, both master and consort displayed the manner of achieving the unified vajra body on the vidyadhara level of life mastery. Mandarava remained in India and has directly and indirectly brought a tremendous benefit to beings. In Tibet, she appeared miraculously at the great Dharma Wheel of Tramdruk where she exchanged symbolic praises and replies with Guru Rinpoche. The details of this are recorded extensively in the Padma Kathang. An independent life story of Mandarava is found in the collected writings of Orgyen Lingpa. Mandarava was a wisdom dakini among whose different names and manifestations are counted the yogini Adorned with Human Bone Ornaments, (Mirükyi Gyenchen), at the time of Lord Marpa, Risülkyi Naljorma at the time of Nyen Lotsawa, and Drubpey Gyalmo at the time of Rechungpa. Mandarava is also accepted as being Chushingi Nyemachen, the consort of Maitripa, as well as the dakini Niguma. Her compassionate emanations and her blessings are beyond any doubt and since she attained the indestructible rainbow body she is surely present (in the world) right now."

MANTRA (sngags). 1) A synonym for Vajrayana. 2) A particular combination of sounds symbolizing and communicating the nature of a deity and which lead to purification and realization, for example OM MANI PADME HUNG. There are chiefly three types of mantra: guhya mantra, vidya mantra and dharani mantra.

MANTRA, VEHICLE OF (sngags; sngags kyi theg pa). Same as Mantrayana. See under Vajrayana.

MANTRAYANA (sngags kyi theg pa). Syn. for Secret Mantra or Vajrayana.

MANTRIKA (sngags pa). A practitioner of Vajrayana.

MARA (bdud). Demon or demonic influence that creates obstacles for practice and enlightenment. Mythologically said be a powerful god who dwells in the highest abode in the Realm of Desire; the master of illusion who attempted to prevent the Buddha from attaining enlightenment at Bodhgaya. For the Dharma practitioner, Mara symbolizes one's own ego-clinging and preoccupation with the eight worldly concerns. Generally, there are four maras or obstructions to practice of the Dharma: those of defilements, death and the aggregates, and the godly mara of seduction. Sometimes the four maras are mentioned by name; Lord of Death, Godly Son, Klesha and Skandha.

MASTER (bla ma). In the *Lamrim Yeshe Nyingpo*, Padmasambhava says: "The vajra master, the root of the path, is someone who has the pure conduct of samaya and vows. He is fully adorned with learning, has discerned it through reflection, and through meditation he possesses the qualities and signs of experience and realization. With his compassionate action he accepts disciples." In short, someone with the correct view and genuine compassion.

MASTER OF UDDIYANA (o rgyan gyi slob dpon). Another name for Padmasambhava.

MEANS AND KNOWLEDGE (thabs dang shes rab; Skt. prajna and upaya). Buddhahood is attained by uniting means and knowledge; in Mahayana, compassion and emptiness, relative and ultimate bodhichitta. In Vajrayana, means and knowledge are the stages of development and completion. According to the Kagyu schools, means refers specifically to the 'path of means,' the Six Doctrines of Naropa and knowledge to the 'path of liberation,' the actual practice of Mahamudra. According to Dzogchen, 'knowledge' is the view of primordial purity, the Trekchö practice of realizing the heart of enlightenment in the present moment, while 'means' is the meditation of spontaneous presence, the Tögal practice of exhausting defilements and fixation through which the rainbow body is realized within one lifetime.

MEDITATION (sgom pa). In the context of Mahamudra or Dzogchen practice, meditation is the act of growing accustomed to or sustaining the continuity of the recognition of our buddha nature as pointed out by a qualified master. In the context of learning, contemplating and meditating, it means the act of assimilating the teachings into one's personal experience, then growing accustomed to them through actual practice.

MILAREPA (mi la ras pa). (1040-1123). One of the most famous yogis and poets in Tibetan religious history. Much of the teachings of the Karma Kagyü schools passed through him. For more details read *The Life of Milarepa* and *The Hundred Thousand Songs of Milarepa* (Shambhala Publications). His name means 'Cotton-clad Mila.'

MIND ONLY SCHOOL (sems tsam pa, Chittamatra). A Mahayana school of Buddhist philosophy propagated by the great master Asanga and his followers. Founded on the Lankavatara Sutra and other scriptures, its main premise is that all phenomena are only mind, i.e. mental perceptions that appear within the all-ground consciousness due to habitual tendencies. Positively, this view relinquishes the fixation on a solid reality. Negatively, there is still clinging to a truly existing 'mind' within which everything takes place.

MIND TERMA (dgongs gter). A revelation directly within the mind of a great master, without the need for a terma of material substance. The teachings revealed in this way were implanted within the 'indestructible sphere' at the time when the master in a former life was one of Padmasambhava's disciples.

MOTHER TANTRA (ma rgyud). One of the three aspects of Anuttara Yoga which places emphasis on completion stage or prajna. Sometimes equivalent to Anu Yoga.

MOUNT SUMERU AND THE FOUR CONTINENTS MOUNT SUMERU (ri rab lhun po gling bzhi dang bcas pa). The mythological giant mountain at the center of our world-system surrounded by the four continents, where the two lowest classes of gods of the Desire Realm live. It is encircled by chains of lesser mountains, lakes, continents, and oceans and is said to rise 84,000 leagues above sea-level. Our present world is situated on the southern continent called Jambudvipa.

NADI (rtsa). The channels in the vajra body through which the energy currents move.

NADI-KNOTS (rtsa mdud). Sometimes the equivalent of chakra, a major junction or meeting point of channels, sometimes a subtle blockage that needs to be untied through yogic practices.

NAMKHAI NYINGPO OF NUB (gnubs nam mkha'i snying po). Born in the district of Lower Nyal, he was one of the first Tibetans to take ordination. An adept translator, he journeyed to India where he received transmission from Hungkara and attained the body of nondual wisdom. Namkhai Nyingpo is also counted among the twenty-five disciples of Guru Rinpoche. Receiving the transmission of Vishuddha Mind, he became able to fly on the rays of the sun. When meditating in Splendid Long Cave of Kharchu at Lhodrak he had visions of numerous yidams and attained the vidyadhara level of mahamudra. Eventually he departed for celestial realms without leaving a corpse behind. Namkhai Nyingpo means 'essence of space.'

NANAM YESHE, alias Yeshe Dey of Nanam (sna nam ye shes sde). Also known as Bandey Yeshe Dey of Shang (zhang gi bhan dhe ye shes sde). A prolific translator of more than 200 scriptures and a disciple of Padmasambhava, this learned and accomplished monk once exhibited his miraculous powers, attained through mastery of Vajra Kilaya, by soaring through the sky like a bird. Yeshe mean 'original wakefulness.'

NIHILISM (chad lta). Literally, 'the view of discontinuance.' The extreme view of nothing-ness: no rebirth or karmic effects, and the nonexistence of a mind after death.

NINE GRADUAL VEHICLES (theg pa rim pa dgu). Shravaka, Pratyekabuddha, Bodhisattva, Kriya, Upa, Yoga, Maha Yoga, Anu Yoga, and Ati Yoga. The first two are Hinayana; the third is Mahayana; the next three are the Three Outer Tantras; and the last three are called the Three Inner Tantras.

NINE SERENE STATES OF SUCCESSIVE ABIDING (mthar gyis gnas pa'i snyoms par 'jug pa dgu). The four dhyanas, the four formless states, and the shravaka's samadhi of peace, also known as the serenity of cessation.

NIRMANAKAYA (sprul sku). 'Emanation body,' 'form of magical apparition.' The third of the three kayas. The aspect of enlightenment that can be perceived by ordinary beings.

NONARISING NATURE OF MIND (sems nyid skye ba med pa). In the aspect of ultimate truth, all phenomena are devoid of an independent, concrete identity and have therefore no basis for such attributes as 'arising, dwelling or ceasing' i.e. coming into being, remain-ing in time and place, and ceasing to exist.

NONTHOUGHT (mi rtog pa). See 'bliss, clarity and nonthought.'

NYANG RAL (nyang ral). Short for Nyang Ral Nyima Özer.

NYANG RAL NYIMA ÖZER (nyang ral nyi ma 'od zer). (1124-1192). The first of the Five Tertön Kings and a reincarnation of King Trisong Deutsen. Several of his revealed treasures are included in the Rinchen Terdzö, among which the most well known is the Kagye Deshek Düpa, a cycle of teachings focusing on the Eight Sadhana Teachings, and the biography of Guru Rinpoche called *Sanglingma*, now published as *The Lotus-born* (Shambhala). Nyang Ral means 'Braided one from Nyang,' and Nyima Özer means 'Ray of sun light.'

NYINGTIG YABZHI (snying thig ya bzhi). One of the most famous collections of Dzogchen scriptures. Vimalamitra united the two aspects of Innermost Unexcelled Section — the explanatory lineage with scriptures and the hearing lineage without scriptures — and concealed them to be revealed as the Nyingtig teachings Vima Nyingtig, and also as the Secret Heart Essence of Vimalamitra (bi ma'i gsang ba snying thig). Longchenpa clarified them in his 51 sections of Lama Yangtig. Padmakara concealed his teachings on the Innermost Unexcelled Cycle to be revealed in the future as Khandro Nyingtig, the Heart Essence of the Dakinis. Longchenpa also clarified these teachings in his Khandro Yangtig. These four exceptional sets of Dzogchen instructions are, together with Longchenpa's addi-tional teachings Zabmo Yangtig, contained in his collection, Nyingtig Yabshi.

ORIGINAL WAKEFULNESS (ye shes). Usually translated as 'wisdom.' Basic cognizance in-dependent of intellectual constructs.

PADMA GARWANG LODRÖ THAYE (padma gar dbang blo gros mtha' yas). Another name for Jam-gön Kongtrül. Padma Garwang means 'Lotus Lord of the Dance,' and Lodrö Thaye means 'Boundless Wisdom.'

PALGYI DORJE (Wangchuk) of Lhalung alias Lhalung Palgyi Dorje (lha lung dpal gyi rdo rje). Born in Upper Drom, he served as a border guard but developed renunciation and to-gether with his two brothers received ordination from Vimalamitra. He received the bodhisattva vow from Padmasambhava as well as empowerment and oral instructions in

Vajrayana. He practiced meditation in the White Gorge of Tsib and at Yerpa, where he reached the accomplishment of being able to move freely through solid rock. Years later he assassinated the evil king Langdarma. Palgyi Dorje means 'Resplendent Vajra.'

PALGYI SENGE OF LANG (rlangs dpal gyi seng ge). His father was Amey Jangchub Drekhöl, a mantrika powerful enough to employ the eight classes of gods and demons as his servants. Palgyi Senge of Lang was one of the eight chief disciples of Padmasambhava when the empowerment of the Assemblage of Sugatas was conferred. He attained both the common and supreme accomplishments at Paro Taktsang through the practice of the Tamer of All Haughty Spirits. The Dzogchen Rinpoches are regarded as his reincarnations. Palgyi Senge means 'Glorious Lion.'

PALGYI SENGE OF SHUBU (shud bu dpal gyi seng ge). One of the ministers of King Trisong Deutsen, sent among the first emissaries to invite Padmasambhava to Tibet. He learned translation from Padmasambhava and rendered numerous teachings of Mamo, Yamantaka and Kilaya into Tibetan. Having attained accomplishment through Kilaya and Mamo, he could split boulders and divide the flow of rivers with his dagger. His reincarnations include the great Tertön Mingyur Dorje of the Namchö tradition. Palgyi Senge means 'Glorious Lion.'

PALGYI WANGCHUK OF KHARCHEN (mkhar chen dpal gyi dbang phyug). In the *Sanglingma* biography he is the father of Yeshe Tsogyal; elsewhere he is described as her brother, a close disciple of Padmasambhava who attained siddhi through the practice of Vajra Kilaya. Palgyi Wangchuk means 'Resplendent Lord.'.

PALGYI WANGCHUK OF O-DREN ('o dran dpal gyi dbang phyug). A great scholar and tantrika, he attained siddhi through practicing Guru Drakpo, the wrathful aspect of Padmasambhava. Palgyi Wangchuk means 'Resplendent Lord.'

PALGYI YESHE OF SOGPO (sog po dpal gyi ye shes). Disciple of Padmasambhava and Jnana Kumara of Nyag. Palgyi Yeshe means 'Glorious Wisdom.'

PANDITA (mkhas pa). A learned master, scholar or professor in Buddhist philosophy.

PARAMITA (pha rol tu phyin pa). Literally, 'paramita' means 'reaching the other shore.' Particularly, it means transcending concepts of subject, object and action. The Paramita vehicle (phar phyin gyi theg pa) is the Mahayana system of the gradual path through the five paths and ten bhumis according to the Prajnaparamita scriptures. See also 'six paramitas.'

PATH OF ACCUMULATION (tshogs lam). The first of the five paths which forms the foundation for the journey towards liberation and involves gathering a vast accumulation of merit dedicated towards this attainment. On this path one gains an intellectual and conceptual understanding of egolessness through learning and reflection. By means of cultivating the four applications of mindfulness, the four right endeavors, and the four legs of miraculous action, one succeeds in eliminating the gross defilements that cause samsaric suffering and in attaining the virtuous qualities of the superknowledges and the 'samadhi of the stream of Dharma' leading to the path of joining.

PATH OF CONSUMMATION (thar phyin pa'i lam). The fifth of the five paths and the state of complete and perfect enlightenment.

PATH OF CULTIVATION (sgom lam). The fourth of the five paths on which one cultivates and trains in the higher practices of a bodhisattva, especially the eight aspects of the path of noble beings.

PATH OF SEEING (mthong lam). The third of the five paths which is the attainment of the first bhumi, liberation from samsara and realization of the truth of reality.

PATHS (lam). See under 'five paths.'

PEMA LEDREL TSAL (padma las 'brel rtsal) (1291-1315). The reincarnation of Pema Sal, the daughter of King Trisong Deutsen. The revealer of the Dzogchen teachings of Guru Rinpoche renowned as *Khandro Nyingtig*. His immediate rebirth was as Longchenpa. Pema Ledrel Tsal means 'Lotus Power of Karmic Link.'

PEMA SAL, PRINCESS (lha lcam padma sal). The daughter of King Trisong Deutsen, to whom Padmasambhava entrusted his own lineage of the Great Perfection known as *Khandro Nyingtig*. She died at an early age, after which Padmasambhava miraculously called her back to life. When her father asked why someone with the great merit to be both a princess and a disciple of the Lotus-Born master had to die while still a child, Padmasambhava told the story of how she had been a bee who stung one of the four brothers during the completion of the Great Stupa of Boudhanath. Pema Sal means 'Radiant Lotus.'

PERCEPTION-SPHERE (skye mched). A state of meditative absorption, possibly lasting many aeons. See under 'Formless Realms.'

PHILOSOPHICAL VEHICLES (mtshan nyid kyi theg pa). A collective name for Hinayana and Mahayana; includes the three vehicles for shravakas, pratyekabuddhas, and bodhisattvas.

POINTING-OUT INSTRUCTION (ngo sprod). The direct introduction to the nature of mind. A root guru is the master who gives the 'pointing-out instruction' so that the disciple recognizes the nature of mind.

PRAJNA AND UPAYA (thabs dang shes rab). Prajna is knowledge or intelligence; in particular, the knowledge of realizing egolessness. Upaya is the method or technique that brings about realization. See also under 'means and knowledge.'

PRANA-MIND (rlung sems). Prana here is the 'wind of karma' and 'mind' the dualistic consciousness of an unenlightened being. These two are closely related.

PRATYEKABUDDHA (rang rgyal, rang sangs rgyas). 'Solitarily Enlightened One.' A Hinayana Arhant who attains Nirvana chiefly through contemplation on the twelve links of dependent origination in reverse order, without needing teachings in that lifetime. He lacks the complete realization of a buddha and so cannot benefit limitless sentient beings as a buddha does.

PRECIOUS HUMAN BODY (mi lus rin po che). Comprised of the eight freedoms and ten riches. The freedoms are to avoid rebirth in the eight unfree states: three lower realms, a long-living god, having wrong views, a savage, a mute, or born in an age without buddhas. The riches are five from oneself and ten from others. The five riches from oneself are: to be a human, centrally born, with intact sense powers, having unperverted livelihood and faith in the right place. The five riches from others are: a buddha appeared and he taught the Dharma, the teachings remain and have followers and (teachers) who compassionately benefit others.

PRELIMINARIES (sngon 'gro). The general outer preliminaries are the Four Mind Changings: reflections on precious human body, impermanence and death, cause and effect of karma, and the shortcomings of samsaric existence. The special inner preliminaries are the Four Times Hundred Thousand Practices of refuge and bodhichitta, Vajrasattva recitation, mandala offering, and guru yoga. See *Torch of Certainty* (Shambhala Publications), and *The Great Gate* (Rangjung Yeshe Publications).

PRINCE MURUB (lha sras mu rúb). The second son of King Trisong Deutsen.

PURE ABODES (gnas gtsang ma). The five highest heavens among the 17 abodes of the Realms of Form. They are called 'pure' because only noble beings, achievers of the path of seeing, can take birth there. Rebirth here is caused by a pure training in the fourth dhyana depending upon whether this cultivation is lesser, medium, great, greater, or extremely great.

PURE PERCEPTION (dag snang). The Vajrayana principle of regarding the environment as a buddhafield, self and others as deities, sounds as mantras, and thoughts as the display of wisdom.

RANGNANG / PERSONAL EXPERIENCE (rang snang). Exemplified by the dream experience, this term is sometimes translated as 'one's own projection' or 'self-display.'

REALMS OF DESIRE ('dod khams). Comprised of the abodes of hell beings, hungry ghosts, animals, humans, asuras, and the gods of the six abodes of Desire gods. It is called 'desire realm' because the beings there are tormented by the mental pain of desire and attachment to material substance.

REALMS OF FORM (gzugs khams). Seventeen samsaric heavenly abodes consisting of the threefold four Dhyana Realms and the five Pure Abodes. A subtle divine state of samsaric existence between the desire realm and the formless realm, where sense of smell, sense of taste and sexual organs are absent. The beings there have bodies of light, long lives and no painful sensations. Unwholesome mental factors such as attachment cannot arise.

RESULTANT VEHICLES ('bras bu'i theg pa). Same as Vajrayana. For details, see 'causal and resultant vehicles.'

RIGDZIN GÖDEM (rig 'dzin rgod kyi ldem phru can). Alias Ngödrub Gyaltsen (dngos grub rgyal mtshan), (1337-1408). The great treasure revealer of the Jangter Tradition. Among his termas are the Dzogchen teachings Kadag Rangjung Rangshar and the better known Gongpa Sangtal. When he was 12 years old three vulture feathers grew on his head, and five more when he was 24. He passed away at the age of 71 amidst miraculous signs. Rigdzin Gödem means 'Vidyadhara Vulture Feathers.'

RIGDZIN GÖKYI DEMTRU CHEN (rig 'dzin rgod kyi ldem phru can). Same as 'Rigdzin Gödem.'

RINCHEN CHOK OF MA (rma rin chen mchog). Early Tibetan translator, among the first seven Tibetans to take ordination from Shantarakshita and the chief recipient of the Magical Net of Mahayoga. He is known for translating the Essence of Secrets Guhyagarbha Tantra, the chief tantra of Mahayoga. Through the teachings he received from Padmasambhava he attained the level of a vidyadhara. Rinchen Chok means 'Sublime Jewel.'

RINCHEN TERDZÖ (rin chen gter mdzod). 'The Great Treasury of Precious Termas,' a collection of the most important revealed termas of Padmasambhava, Vimalamitra, Vairochana and their closest disciples, gathered by Jamgön Kongtrül Lodrö Thaye with the help of Jamyang Khyentse Wangpo. Published in 63 volumes by His Holiness Dilgo Khyentse Rinpoche, New Delhi, India, with the addition of several more volumes of termas and commentaries. Khakyab Dorje, the 15th Karmapa, described it is these words: "The great *Treasury of Precious Termas* is the quintessence of the ocean-like teachings of the sugatas (buddhas), the profound *Vidyadhara Pitaka* of the Early Translation School."

RIPENING AND LIBERATION (smin grol). Two vital parts of Vajrayana practice: the empowerments which ripen one's being with the capacity to realize the four kayas and the liberating oral instructions enabling one to actually apply the insight introduced through the empowerments.

RONGZOMPA, Rongzom Pandita, Chökyi Sangpo (rong zom pa chos kyi bzang po). (1012-1088). Together with Longchenpa, he is regarded as the Nyingma scholar of outstanding brilliance.

ROOTS OF VIRTUE (dge ba'i rtsa ba). A good deed; a moment of renunciation, compassion, or faith. Virtuous deeds created in the present or in former lives.

SADHANA (sgrub thabs). 'Means of accomplishment.' Tantric liturgy and procedure for practice usually emphasizing the development stage. The typical sadhana structure involves a preliminary part including the taking of refuge and arousing bodhichitta, a main part involving visualization of a buddha and recitation of the mantra, and a concluding part with dedication of merit to all sentient beings.

SAHA WORLD (mi mjed kyi 'jig rten) Our known world system; the 'World of Endurance,' because the sentient beings here endure unbearable suffering. Saha can also mean 'Undivided' because the karmas and disturbing emotions, causes and effects, are not separately divided or differentiated.

SAMADHI (ting nge 'dzin). 'Adhering to the continuity of evenness.' A state of undistracted concentration or meditative absorption which in the context of Vajrayana can refer to either the development stage or the completion stage.

SAMANTABHADRA (kun tu bzang po). The 'Ever-excellent One.' 1) The primordial dharmakaya buddha. 2) The bodhisattva Samantabhadra used as the example for the perfection of increasing an offering infinitely.

SAMAYA (dam tshig). The sacred pledges, precepts or commitments of Vajrayana practice. Samayas essentially consist of outwardly, maintaining harmonious relationship with the vajra master and one's Dharma friends and, inwardly, not straying from the continuity of the practice. At the end of a chapter, the single word 'samaya' is an oath that confirms that what has been stated is true.

SAMBHOGAKAYA (longs spyod rdzogs pa'i sku). The 'body of perfect enjoyment.' In the context of the 'five kayas of fruition,' sambhogakaya is the semi-manifest form of the buddhas endowed with the 'five perfections' of perfect teacher, retinue, place, teaching and time which is perceptible only to bodhisattvas on the ten levels.

SAMYE (bsam yas). The wondrous temple complex, modeled after the Indian monastery Odantapuri, built by King Trisong Deutsen (790-844) and consecrated by Guru Rinpoche in 814. A major center of the early transmission of Buddhism in Tibet. It is situated in Central Tibet close to Lhasa. It is also known as Glorious Temple of Samye, the Unchanging and Spontaneously Fulfillment of Boundless Wishes. Its three stories are of Indian, Chinese and Tibetan designs. See *The Lotus-born* (Shambhala Publications).

SAMYE CHIMPHU (bsam yas chims phu). The sacred place of Padmasambhava's speech. A mountain retreat situated four hours walk above Samye. During the last twelve centuries numerous great masters have meditated in the caves at this hermitage.

SANGYE LINGPA (sangs rgyas gling pa). (1340-1396). A reincarnation of the second son of King Trisong Deutsen; a major tertön and revealer of the Lama Gongdü cycle in 13 volumes. Sangye Lingpa means 'Sanctuary of Awakening.'

SANGYE YESHE OF NUB (gnubs sangs rgyas ye shes). One of the twenty-five disciples of Padmasambhava, he was the chief recipient of the Anu Yoga teachings as well as the Yamantaka of Mahayoga. In addition to Guru Rinpoche, his other teachers were Traktung Nagpo and Chögyal Kyong of India, Vasudhara of Nepal, and Chetsen Kye from the country of Drusha. He visited India and Nepal seven times. When the evil king Langdarma attempted to destroy Buddhism in Tibet, Sangye Yeshe instilled fear in the king by causing an enormous scorpion, the size of nine yaks, to magically appear by a single gesture of his right hand. Through this, Langdarma lost the courage to persecute the Vajrayana sangha. Tulku Urgyen Rinpoche is considered one of his reincarnations. Sangye Yeshe means 'Buddha Wisdom.'

SECRET MANTRA (gsang sngags, Skt. guhyamantra). Synonymous with Vajrayana or tantric teachings. 'Guhya' means secret, both concealed and self-secret. 'Mantra' in this context means eminent, excellent, or praiseworthy.

SELF-ENTITY (rang bzhin). An inherently existent and independent entity of the individual self or of phenomena.

SELF-NATURE (rang bzhin). See 'Self-entity.'

SENGCHEN NAMTRAK (seng chen nams brag). One of the 25 sacred places of Kham opened by Chokgyur Lingpa. Sengchen Namtrak means 'Great Lion Sky Cliff.'

SENSE BASES (skye mched). The twelve sense factors are the organs of eye, ear, nose, tongue, body and mind consciousness as well as their corresponding objects which are visual form, sound, smell, taste, texture, and mental object.

SERENITY OF CESSATION ('gog pa'i snyoms 'jug). The meditative state entered by an arhant after all disturbing emotions, sensations and thinking have ceased. It is not considered the ultimate goal by the Mahayana schools.

SEVEN LINE SUPPLICATION (tshig bdun gsol 'debs). The famous supplication to Padmasambhava beginning with "On the northwest border of the country of Uddiyana, ..."

SEVEN WAYS OF TRANSMISSION (bka' babs bdun). Canonical or oral lineage, revealed treasure, rediscovered treasure, mind treasure, recollection, pure vision and hearing lineage.

SEVENFOLD PURITY (dag pa bdun). Same as the seven branches: Prostrating, making offerings, confessing, rejoicing, requesting to turn the Wheel of the Dharma, beseeching not to pass into nirvana, and dedicating the merit for the welfare of all beings.

SHAMATHA (zhi gnas) 'calm abiding' or 'remaining in quiescence' after thought activity has subsided; or, the meditative practice of calming the mind in order to rest free from the disturbance of thought.

SHRAMANA (dge sbyong). A spiritual practitioner. Often has the connotation of an ascetic or mendicant monk.

SHRAVAKA (nyan thos). 'Hearer' or 'listener.' Hinayana practitioner of the First Turning of the Wheel of the Dharma on the four noble truths who realizes the suffering inherent in samsara, and focuses on understanding that there is no independent self. By conquering disturbing emotions, he liberates himself, attaining first the stage of Stream Enterer at the Path of Seeing, followed by the stage of Once-Returner who will be reborn only one more time, and the stage of Non-returner who will no longer be reborn into samsara. The final goal is to become an Arhant. These four stages are also known as the 'four results of spiritual practice.'

SHRI GUHYASAMAJA (dpal gsang ba 'dus pa). Literally, 'Assembly of Secrets.' One of the major tantras and yidams of the New School.

SHRI SINGHA (Skt). The chief disciple and successor of Manjushrimitra in the lineage of the Dzogchen teachings. He was born in the city of Shokyam in Khotan and studied with the masters Hatibhala and Bhelakirti. Among Shri Singha's disciples were four outstanding masters: Jnanasutra, Vimalamitra, Padmasambhava and the Tibetan translator Vairochana.

SHURMA (shur ma). A Tibetan script, half way between printed and written script.

SINDHURA (Skt.). Red or deep orange substance often used in tantric rituals.

SIX CLASSES OF BEINGS ('gro ba rigs drug). Gods, demigods, human beings, animals, hungry ghosts, and hell beings.

SIX LIMITS (mtha' drug). The views of the expedient and definitive meaning, the implied and the not implied, the literal and the not literal. Together with the 'four modes' they form the indispensable keys for unlocking the meaning of the tantras.

SIX PARAMITAS (phar phyin drug). The six transcendent actions of generosity, discipline, patience, diligence, concentration, and discriminating knowledge.

SIX SUPERKNOWLEDGES (mngon par shes pa drug). The capacities for performing miracles, divine sight, divine hearing, recollection of former lives, cognition of the minds of others, and the cognition of the exhaustion of defilements.

SUKHAVATI (bde ba can). See 'Blissful Realm.'

SUTRA (mdo, mdo sde). 1) A discourse by or inspired by the Buddha. 2) A scripture of the Sutra pitaka within the Tripitaka. 3) All exoteric teachings of Buddhism belonging to Hinayana and Mahayana, the causal teachings that regard the path as the cause of enlightenment, as opposed to the esoteric, tantric teachings.

SUTRA ON THE FURTHERANCE OF VIRTUE (mdo dge rgyas).

SUTRA PITAKA (mdo'i sde snod). See under 'Sutra.'

SUTRA REQUESTED BY UNENDING INTELLIGENCE (blo gros mi zad pas zhus pa'i mdo).

TANTRA (rgyud). The Vajrayana teachings given by the Buddha in his sambhogakaya form. The real sense of tantra is 'continuity,' the innate buddha nature, which is known as the 'tantra of the expressed meaning.' The general sense of tantra is the extraordinary tantric scriptures also known as the 'tantra of the expressing words.' Can also refer to all the resultant teachings of Vajrayana as a whole.

TANTRA OF THE IMMACULATE KING OF CONFESSION (dri med bshags rgyud kyi rgyal po).

TARPALING IN BUMTANG ('bum thang thar pa gling). Temple in eastern Bhutan founded by Longchen Rabjam.

TAWA LONG-YANG (lta ba klong yangs). A treasure cycle of the Father Tantra aspect of the Great Perfection revealed by Dorje Lingpa (1346-1405). Tawa Long-yang means 'Vast Expanse of the View.'

TEN NONVIRTUES (mi dge ba bcu). The physical misdeeds are killing, taking what is not given, and engaging in sexual misconduct. The verbal misdeeds are lying, uttering divisive talk, harsh words, and gossiping. The mental misdeeds are harboring covetousness, ill-will, and wrong views.

TEN SPIRITUAL ACTIVITIES (chos spyod bcu). Copying scriptures, making offerings, giving alms, listening to discourses, memorizing, reading, expounding, reciting, reflecting upon and training in the meaning of the Dharma.

TEN TOPICS OF TANTRA (rgyud kyi dngos po bcu). View, conduct, mandala, empowerment, samaya, activity, accomplishment, samadhi, offering puja, mantra and mudra. These are the ten aspects of the path of a tantric practitioner, as well as the ten primary topics to be explained.

TEN VIRTUES (dge ba bcu). Generally, to refrain from the above ten nonvirtues. In particular, to engage in their opposites; for example, to save life, be generous, etc.

TENGAM (rten gam). Room of sacred objects.

TENMA GODDESSES or Twelve Tenma Goddesses (brtan ma bcu gnyis). Important female protectors of the Nyingma lineage, semi-mundane semi-wisdom protectors.

TENTH DAY PRACTICE IN EIGHT CHAPTERS (tshe bcu le'u brgyad pa).

TERMA (gter ma). 'Treasure.' 1) The transmission through concealed treasures hidden, mainly by Guru Rinpoche and Yeshe Tsogyal, to be discovered at the proper time by a 'tertön,' a treasure revealer, for the benefit of future disciples. It is one of the two chief traditions of the Nyingma School, the other being 'Kama.' This tradition is said to continue even long after the Vinaya of the Buddha has disappeared. 2) Concealed treasures of many different kinds, including texts, ritual objects, relics, and natural objects.

TERTÖN (gter ston). A revealer of hidden treasures, concealed mainly by Guru Rinpoche and Yeshe Tsogyal.

TESTAMENT OF PADMA (padma'i bka' chems). Revealed by the great tertön Nyang Ral, and presumably identical with the medium-length version of the *Sanglingma* biography of Padmasambhava, an English translation of which is published as *The Lotus-Born* (Shambhala Publications, 1993).

THREE DOORS (sgo gsum). Body, speech and mind; thought, word and deed.

THREE JEWELS (dkon mchog gsum). The Precious Buddha, the Precious Dharma and the Precious Sangha. In *The Light of Wisdom* (Shambhala Publ.), Jamgön Kongtrül explains: "The Buddha is the nature of the four kayas and five wisdoms endowed with the twofold purity and the perfection of the twofold welfare. The Dharma is what is expressed, the unconditioned truth of total purification comprised of cessation and path, and that which expresses, the two aspects of statement and realization appearing as the names, words and letters of the teachings. The Sangha consists of the actual Sangha, the sons of the victorious ones abiding on the noble bhumis who are endowed with the qualities of wisdom and liberation, and the resembling Sangha who are on the paths of accumulation and joining as well as the noble shravakas and pratyekabuddhas."

THREE KAYAS (sku gsum). Dharmakaya, sambhogakaya and nirmanakaya. The three kayas as ground are 'essence, nature, and expression,' as path they are 'bliss, clarity and non-thought,' and as fruition they are the 'three kayas of buddhahood.' The three kayas of buddhahood are the dharmakaya which is free from elaborate constructs and endowed with the 'twenty-one sets of enlightened qualities;' the sambhogakaya which is of the nature of light and endowed with the perfect major and minor marks perceptible only to bodhisattvas on the levels; and the nirmanakaya which manifests in forms perceptible to both pure and impure beings.

THREE ROOTS (rtsa ba gsum). Guru, Yidam and Dakini. The Guru is the root of blessings, the Yidam of accomplishment, and the Dakini of activity.

THREE SETS OF VOWS (sdom pa gsum). The Hinayana vows of individual liberation, the Mahayana trainings of a bodhisattva, and the Vajrayana samayas of a vidyadhara, a tantric practitioner.

THREEFOLD EXCELLENCE (dam pa gsum). The excellent beginning of bodhichitta, the excellent main part without conceptualization and the excellent conclusion of dedication. Also called the three excellencies. For a detailed explanation, see *Repeating the Words of the Buddha* (Rangjung Yeshe Publ.).

TIDRO CAVE AT SHOTÖ (sho stod sti sgro). Sacred place of Padmasambhava and Yeshe Tsogyal near Drigung Til in Central Tibet. Opened by Padmasambhava for future practitioners, this important pilgrimage site also has hot springs with healing properties.

TORMA (gtor ma). An implement used in tantric ceremonies. Can also refer to a food offering to protectors of the Dharma or unfortunate spirits.

TREASURY OF PRECIOUS TERMAS (rin chen gter mdzod). See under 'Rinchen Terdzö.'

TRIPITAKA (sde snod gsum). The three collections of the teachings of Buddha Shakyamuni: Vinaya, Sutra, and Abhidharma. Their purpose is the development of the three trainings of discipline, concentration and discriminating knowledge while their function is to remedy the three poisons of desire, anger and delusion. The Tibetan version of the Tripitaka fills more than one hundred large volumes, each with more than 600 large pages. In a wider sense all of the Dharma, both Sutra and Tantra, is contained within the three collections and three trainings. To paraphrase Khenpo Ngakchung in his *Notes to the Preliminary Practices for Longchen Nyingtig:* "The three collections of Hinayana scriptures, namely Vinaya, Sutra, and Abhidharma, respectively express the meaning of the training in discipline, concentration and discriminating knowledge. The teachings describing the details of precepts for the bodhisattva path belong to the Vinaya collection while the meaning expressed by these scriptures are the training in discipline. The sutras expressing the gateways to samadhi are the Sutra collection while their expressed meaning, reflections on precious human body and so forth, are the training in concentration. The scriptures on the sixteen or twenty types of emptiness are the Abhidharma collection while their expressed meaning is the training in discriminating knowledge. Scriptures expounding the details of the samayas of Vajrayana are the Vinaya collection while their expressed meaning is the training in discipline. The scriptures teaching the general points of development and completion belong to the Sutra collection, while their expressed meaning is the training in samadhi. All the scriptures expressing the Great Perfection belong to the Abhidharma collection, while their expressed meaning is the training in discriminating knowledge."

TRISONG DEUTSEN (khri srong de'u btsan). (790-844) The second great Dharma king of Tibet who invited Guru Rinpoche, Shantarakshita, Vimalamitra, and many other Buddhist teachers including Jinamitra and Danashila. In *The Precious Garland of Lapis Lazuli*, Jamgön Kongtrül dates Trisong Deutsen as being born on the eighth day of the third month of spring in the year of the Male Water Horse (802). Other sources state that year as his enthronement upon the death of his father. Until the age of seventeen he was chiefly engaged in ruling the kingdom. He built Samye, the great monastery and teaching center modeled after Odantapuri, established Buddhism as the state religion of Tibet, and during his reign the first monks were ordained. He arranged for panditas and lotsawas to translate innumerable sacred texts, and he established a large number of centers for teaching and practice. Among his later incarnations are Nyang Ral Nyima Özer (1124-1192), Guru Chöwang (1212-1270), Jigmey Lingpa (1729-1798), and Jamyang Khyentse Wangpo (1820-1892).

TRÖMA NAGMO (khros ma nag mo). A wrathful black form of the female buddha Vajra Yogini. Tröma Nagmo means 'Black Lady of Wrath.'

TSEN (btsan). A type of evil spirit.

TSOGYAL (mtsho rgyal). See under 'Yeshe Tsogyal.'

TUKDRUB BARCHEY KÜNSEL (thugs sgrub bar chad kun sel). A cycle of teachings revealed by Chokgyur Lingpa together with Jamyang Khyentse Wangpo consisting of about ten volumes of texts. Belong to the principle of Guru Vidyadhara. For details, see foreword to *The Great Gate* (Rangjung Yeshe Publ.). Tukdrub means 'Heart practice,' Barchey Künsel means 'dispeller of all obstacles.'

TULKU URGYEN RINPOCHE (sprul sku u rgyan rin po che). A contemporary master of the Kagyü and Nyingma lineages, who lives at Nagi Gompa in Nepal.

TWO ACCUMULATIONS (tshogs gnyis). The accumulation of merit with concepts and the accumulation of wisdom beyond concepts.

TWO OBSCURATIONS (sgrib gnyis). The obscuration of disturbing emotions and the cognitive obscuration.

TWO TRUTHS (bden pa gnyis). Relative truth and ultimate truth. Relative truth describes the seeming, superficial and apparent mode of all things. Ultimate truth describes the real, true and unmistaken mode. These two aspects of reality are defined by the Four Philosophical Schools as well as the tantras of Vajrayana in different ways, each progressively deeper and closer to describing things as they are.

UDUMVARA (Skt.) 'Especially eminent' or 'supremely exalted.' This flower is said to appear and bloom only accompanying the appearance of a fully enlightened buddha.

UPASAKA (dge bsnyen). A Buddhist layman, bound by the five vows to avoid killing, stealing, lying, sexual misconduct, and intoxicating liquor. The Tibetan equivalent, *genyen*, means 'pursuer of virtue.'

UPAYA (thabs). See 'means and knowledge.'

VAIROCHANA (Skt.). The great translator who lived during the reign of King Trisong Deutsen. Among the first seven Tibetan monks, he was sent to India to study with Shri Singha. Along with Padmasambhava and Vimalamitra, he was one of the three main masters to bring the Dzogchen teachings to Tibet.

VAJRA BODY (rdo rje'i lus / sku). The human body, the subtle channels of which resemble the structure of a vajra.

VAJRA HELL (rdo rje'i myal ba). The lowest hell of Incessant Pain.

VAJRA SEAT (rdo rje gdan, Skt. vajrasana). The 'diamond throne' under the Bodhi Tree in Bodhgaya where Buddha Shakyamuni attained enlightenment.

VAJRA TÖTRENG (rdo rje thod phreng). 'Vajra Garland of skulls.' One of Padmasambhava's names.

VAJRA-HOLDER (rdo rje 'dzin pa). 1) Respectful title for an accomplished master. 2) The state of enlightenment.

VAJRADHARA (rdo rje 'chang). 'Vajra-holder.' The dharmakaya buddha of the Sarma Schools. Can also refer to one's personal teacher of Vajrayana or to the all-embracing buddha nature.

VAJRADHATU MANDALA (rdo rje dbyings kyi dkyil 'khor). An important sadhana of Mahayoga containing the 42 peaceful deities.

VAJRAKAYA (rdo rje'i sku). The unchanging quality of the buddha nature. Sometimes counted among the five kayas of buddhahood.

VAJRAPANI (phyag na rdo rje). 'Vajra Bearer.' One of the eight great bodhisattvas and the chief compiler of the Vajrayana teachings. Also known as 'Lord of Secrets.'

VAJRAYANA (rdo rje theg pa). The 'vajra vehicle.' The practices of taking the result as the path. Same as 'Secret Mantra.'

VIDYADHARA (rig pa 'dzin pa). 'Knowledge-holder.' Holder (*dhara*) or bearer of knowledge (*vidya*) mantra. A realized master on one of the four stages on the tantric path of Mahayoga, the tantric equivalent of the eleven levels. Another definition is: Bearer of the profound method, the knowledge which is the wisdom of deity, mantra and great bliss.

VIEW, MEDITATION, CONDUCT AND FRUITION (lta ba sgom pa spyod pa 'bras bu). The philosophical orientation, the act of growing accustomed to that — usually in sitting practice, the implementation of that insight during the activities of daily life, and the final outcome resulting from such training. Each of the nine vehicles has its particular definition of view, meditation, conduct and fruition.

VIMALAMITRA (dri med bshes gnyen). A Dzogchen master who was invited to Tibet by King Trisong Deutsen. One of the three main forefathers of the Dzogchen teachings, especially Nyingtig, in Tibet. Vimalamitra means 'Flawless Kinsman.'

VINAYA ('dul ba). 'Discipline.' One of the three parts of the Tripitaka. The Buddha's teachings showing ethics, the discipline and moral conduct that is the foundation for all Dharma practice, both for lay and ordained people.

VINAYA PITAKA ('dul ba'i sde snod). See 'Tripitaka.'

VIPASHYANA (lhag mthong). 'Clear' or 'wider seeing.' Usually referring to insight into emptiness. One of the two main aspects of meditation practice, the other being shamatha.

VOWS AND PRECEPTS (bslab sdom). See under 'Three sets of vows.'

WHEEL OF THE DHARMA (chos kyi 'khor lo). To turn the wheel of Dharma is poetic for giving teachings. In specific, the cycle of teachings given by the Buddha; three such cycles,
known as the Three Turnings of the Wheel of the Dharma, were taught by Shakyamuni Buddha during his lifetime.

WISDOM (ye shes). In this book this word is usually translated as 'original wakefulness.'
There are also the five wisdoms, aspects of how the cognitive quality of buddha nature
functions: the dharmadhatu wisdom, mirror-like wisdom, wisdom of equality, discriminating wisdom and all-accomplishing wisdom.

YAMANTAKA (gshin rje gshed). A wrathful form of Manjushri, representing wisdom that sub-
dues death. Among the Eight Sadhana Teachings he is the wrathful buddha of the Body
Family. Yamantaka means 'Slayer of Yama,' the Lord of Death.

YANA (theg pa). 'That which carries,' 'vehicle.' A set of teachings which enable one to journey towards rebirth in the higher realms, liberation from samsara or complete buddhahood.

YESHE TSOGYAL (ye shes mtsho rgyal). The different versions of her biography give varying
details about her place of birth, the names of her parents and so forth. In his Ocean of
Wondrous Sayings to Delight the Learned Ones, Guru Tashi Tobgyal states that her father's name was Namkha Yeshe of the Kharchen clan and that she was born in Drong-
mochey of Drak. At first she was one of King Trisong Deutsen's queens but later was
given to Padmasambhava to be his spiritual consort. During the empowerment of Assemblage of Sugatas, her initiation flower fell on the mandala of Kilaya. Through this
practice she became able to tame evil spirits and revive the dead. She was the chief
compiler of all the inconceivable teachings given by the great master Padmasambhava.
Having remained in Tibet for two hundred years, she departed for the celestial realm of
the Glorious Copper Colored Mountain, without leaving a corpse behind. In *The Precious Garland of Lapis Lazuli*, Jamgön Kongtrül says, "Yeshe Tsogyal was a direct incarnation of Dhatvishvari Vajra Yogini in the form of a woman. She served
Padmasambhava perfectly in that life, engaged in sadhana practice with incredible perseverance and attained a level equal to Padmasambhava himself, the 'continuity adorned
with inexhaustible body, speech, mind, qualities, and activities.' Her kindness to the
land of Tibet surpasses the imagination and her compassionate activity that is no different from Padmasambhava's continues unceasingly." Yeshe Tsogyal means 'Victorious
Ocean of Wisdom.'

YESHE YANG OF BA (sba ye shes dbyangs). Tibetan translator predicted by Padmasambhava.
The chief scribe for writing down the termas of Padmasambhava, he was an accom-
plished yogi, able to fly like a bird to the celestial realms. Also known as Atsara Yeshe
Yang. Yeshe Yang means 'Melodious Wisdom.'

YIDAM (yi dam). A personal deity and the root of accomplishment among the Three Roots.
The yidam is one's tutelary deity; a personal protector of one's practice and guide to

enlightenment. Traditionally, yidam practice is the main practice that follows the preliminaries. It includes the two stages of development and completion and is a perfect stepping stone for, or the bridge to approaching, the more subtle practices of Mahamudra and Dzogchen. Later on, yidam practice is the perfect enhancement for the view of these subtle practices.

YOGA (mal 'byor). 1) The actual integration of learning into personal experience. 2) The third of the three outer tantras: Kriya, Upa and Yoga. It emphasizes the view rather than the conduct and to regard the deity as being the same level as oneself.

YOGIC DISCIPLINE (rtul shugs). Additional practices for a tantrika in order to train in implementing the view of Vajrayana during activities; for example Chö practice in frightening places. It can be pursued by the practitioner who has strong familiarity with the view and stability in meditation practice. Carries the connotation of 'courageous conduct.'